OUR
GUIDE D0563194 TO EVERYDAY LIFE

CLOSER TO
GOD

BOB HOSTETLER

Our Daily Bread
Publishing™

To Aubrey, Kevin, Aaron, Nina
B. H.

Closer to God
© 2019 by Discovery House (Our Daily Bread Publishing)
All rights reserved.

Requests for permission to quote from this book should be directed to: Permissions Department, Our Daily Bread Publishing, PO Box 3566, Grand Rapids, MI 49501, or contact us by email at permissionsdept@odb.org.

Interior design by Michael J. Williams

Library of Congress Cataloging-in-Publication Data

Names: Hostetler, Bob, 1958- author.
Title: Closer to God / Bob Hostetler.
Description: Grand Rapids, Michigan : Discovery House Publishers, [2019] | Series: Our Daily Bread guides to everyday faith | Includes bibliographical references and index.
Identifiers: LCCN 2018061296 | ISBN 9781627079297 (pbk. : alk. paper)
Subjects: LCSH: Spirituality--Christianity. | Spiritual life--Christianity. | Christian life.
Classification: LCC BV4501.3 .H6779 2019 | DDC 248.4--dc23
LC record available at https://lccn.loc.gov/2018061296

Printed in the United States of America
First printing in 2019

"Come close to God, and God will come close to you."

(James 4:8 NLT)

CONTENTS

THE PLANT

Am I the only one?

That's the thought flashing through your mind. You feel a strange uneasiness, sitting in church, looking around, half-listening to the pastor's sermon. A woman catches your glance, and you smile. She smiles back and you turn away, your smile already gone.

People around you are listening attentively to the sermon. Some seem to be taking notes, with a pen or on their phone—unless they're texting or surfing the web. That's always possible. But they look like they're engaged. Rapt, even. And you're thinking about other things.

You know many of the people in the room. Quite a few are friends. Yet you feel as if you exist in a different dimension. They seem happier, more fulfilled. They talk and act as if they're growing and thriving spiritually, much like the green, leafy plants that line the platform. Are those plants real? Or fake? Are they like your friends, or like the way you feel right now? You try to be sincere and open, of course, but honestly, sometimes it feels like you're going through the motions, treading water, faking-it-not-making-it.

Then you notice one plant, the next-to-the-last seedling on the right side. It's looking a little droopy. Bedraggled. Thirsty.

So the plants are real, after all, you think. But that one supplies a fitting metaphor for your spiritual life. You're alive, sure. You have a relationship with God through Jesus Christ, and you have grown over the years—some years more than others, of course. But you have come a long way. And you have occasional glimpses of what a thriving, flourishing, close relationship with God looks and feels like. Still, something's wrong. Something's missing. You feel more like that poor plant than the ones that seem as if they're about to bust out in fragrant flowers.

You're not as close to God as you want to be. Not nearly.

But you want to be. You really do.

Never Hungry, Never Thirsty

Jesus painted quite the picture of the kind of life His followers could expect. He told a woman He met at a well in Samaria, "Whoever drinks the water I give them will never thirst. Indeed, the water I give them will become in them a spring of water welling up to eternal life" (John 4:14). That sounds enticing, doesn't it? He was speaking metaphorically, of course, but if that's not a picture of spiritual affluence, what is?

On another occasion, Jesus said of His followers, "I have come that they may have life, and have it to the full" (John 10:10). What could be clearer? What could be better?

He even claimed, "Whoever comes to me will never go hungry, and whoever believes in me will never be thirsty" (John 6:35). Never hungry? Never thirsty? Again, Christ was using a metaphor, but His meaning seems clear enough. He was speaking of a flourishing spiritual life, the kind we all crave . . . and the kind we often feel like we're missing, somehow.

Were Jesus's claims a kind of bait-and-switch, in which something of great value is promised but a much lesser commodity is delivered? Were His words like a carrot on a stick, which a mule driver hangs in front of the animal to entice it to move forward—a reward it never quite reaches? Is Jesus like Lucy in the classic *Peanuts* comic strips, holding a football for Charlie Brown to kick, only to snatch it away every single time?

I wonder if Jesus's first followers ever felt that way. After all, they knew Jesus; they'd followed Him. They recognized Him as "the Lamb of God, who takes away the sin of the world" (John 1:29) and "the Messiah, the Son of the living God" (Matthew 16:16). But they still had doubts (see Matthew 8:26, 14:31, 16:8). They still argued among themselves (see Mark 9:34, Luke 22:24). They said and did some wildly inappropriate things (see Luke 9:54, John 18:10). And, even after Jesus commissioned them to preach and perform miracles throughout the countryside, they still experienced mystifying moments of powerlessness.

Something Missing, Something Better

Once, a man brought his son to Jesus for healing. The Son of God wasn't there, so the man cornered some of Jesus's closest followers. His son was possessed by a demon, and this desperate father needed help.

So those disciples stepped up and tried to call the demon out of the boy.

And failed.

Then Jesus arrived at the scene. The father explained his son's predicament *and* the disciples' failed efforts. Jesus said, "Bring the boy to me." The account goes on:

> So, they brought him. When the spirit saw Jesus, it immediately threw the boy into a convulsion. He fell to the ground and rolled around, foaming at the mouth.
>
> Jesus asked the boy's father, "How long has he been like this?"
>
> "From childhood," he answered. "It has often thrown him into fire or water to kill him. But if you can do anything, take pity on us and help us."
>
> "'If you can'?" said Jesus. "Everything is possible for one who believes."
>
> Immediately the boy's father exclaimed, "I do believe; help me overcome my unbelief!"
>
> When Jesus saw that a crowd was running to the scene, he rebuked the impure spirit. "You deaf and mute spirit," he said, "I command you, come out of him and never enter him again."
>
> The spirit shrieked, convulsed him violently and came out. The boy looked so much like a corpse that many said, "He's dead." But Jesus

took him by the hand and lifted him to his feet, and he stood up. (Mark 9:20–27)

I'm going to talk more about that encounter with Jesus later in this book (in chapter 4! No peeking . . . unless you want to), but for now I just want to point out to you this:

That was an *amazing* moment for that father and his son. But Jesus's followers found it perplexing. Disconcerting, even. When they got Jesus to themselves later, they asked, "Why couldn't we drive it out?" (Mark 9:28). *What did I do wrong?*, each of them must've been thinking. *Why couldn't I do that? What am I missing?*

Maybe you can identify with those first followers of Jesus. They felt a disconnect between their expectations—even their past experiences—and their reality, a divide between the promises and their fulfillment. Things didn't all come together automatically for them, even after the resurrection—even after the giving of the Holy Spirit on the Day of Pentecost. Much did, of course. Resurrection and regeneration will do that. But even then, the earliest followers of Jesus still learned and grew and, eventually, experienced a closeness to God that utterly transformed them . . . and the world.

And so can you.

CHAPTER ONE

COME, FOLLOW ME

If you and I had been there that day by the Sea of Galilee, we might have seen Simon Bar-Jonah (later called "Peter") in a fishing boat with his brother Andrew. We might have heard Jesus call from the shoreline to the brothers (whom He probably knew already) as they tossed a weighted net into the water: "Come, follow me."

We might have watched as they stopped their sweaty work and tented a hand over their eyes. We may have smelled the fish and heard the lapping of the water on the shore and turned to see Jesus smile as He called again: "I will teach you to fish for people." And we would have joined Peter and

Andrew as they dropped their nets, steered the boat to land, and leaped out to follow him—right? Of course right.

After all, we have left our nets behind—metaphorically speaking—to follow Jesus. Like those first followers, we signed on wholeheartedly and unconditionally. And following Jesus transformed us. We experienced an infusion of new life and became new creations from the inside out. Yet we still feel a disconnect between our expectations and our reality, a divide between the promises and their fulfillment. For all God has done for us, we long to be closer to Him, to experience "a spring of water welling up to eternal life" (John 4:14) and life more abundant (see John 10:10).

That drive to know more of God, that quest for gaining "new heights . . . every day,"[1] as the hymn writer put it, is an important part of what it means to follow Jesus Christ. It isn't wrong to crave "even greater things" (John 14:12) in your life with God. But there is often a cycle that occurs in the life of a person who is sincerely following Jesus, a cycle that may be reflected in the Bible's depiction of Simon Peter's journey from his fishing boat on the Sea of Galilee to his breakfast with Jesus by that same sea, to the Day of Pentecost . . . and beyond.

The Circle of (Spiritual) Life

Many people expect their spiritual lives to progress more or less like a hot-air balloon ride: a fairly steady advance to greater heights and increasingly breath-taking vistas. That seldom happens. You probably already know that.

Many followers of Jesus experience something more akin to a tilt-a-whirl, a dizzying succession of ups, downs, and spins that can be exciting—but also dismaying at times. So it seems to have been in the life of Peter, as recorded in the Bible. The twists and turns he experienced may not only feel familiar to you; they may also help to explain where you are now and prepare you for a new, better, and closer place in your relationship with God. Let's take a look at them now.

The Call

As He did that day beside the Sea of Galilee, Jesus still calls men and women to follow Him. Some hear the call in a worship service and respond by kneeling and praying at an altar. Some hear His invitation while reading a book or listening to a song. Others while praying with a friend. Or washing the dishes. Or driving in the car. Even in school . . . or prison.

Sometimes people respond to Jesus with over-whelming emotion—tears, cries, and trembling.

For others, however, the decision to follow Jesus can be surprisingly unemotional, but intentional and resolute. In some cases, it's sudden, like a clap of thunder, while in other instances it's the culmination of a long, gradual process. In every case, however, as it was in Simon Peter's experience, the Christian life begins by hearing and heeding the call of Jesus: "Follow me."

Enthusiasm

When a human soul experiences new life in Jesus Christ, the experience often brings with it waves of enthusiasm. So much is new and refreshing: forgiveness of sins, an invigorating cleanness of heart, a surfeit of beauty and wonder.

Such was the case, apparently, with Peter. After all, he watched Jesus turn water to wine, feed a crowd of thousands with a pocketful of food, heal the sick, and raise the dead. He even saw Jesus transfigured on a hilltop, where Moses and Elijah performed a kind of air dance with Jesus before Peter's very eyes. Peter blurted, "Lord, this is wonderful! If you want me to, I'll make three shrines, one for you, one for Moses, and one for Elijah" (see Matthew 17:4 NLT).

Do you recall a "This is wonderful!" stage in your spiritual life? Those moments when all seemed new and exciting? When love and joy exuded from you, overflowing onto those around you? Such enthusiasm is thoroughly common for those who experience new life in Christ. It's also an experience that typically leads one further, to commitment.

Commitment

Did Peter know, when he parked his fishing boat at the curb and handed the keys to someone else, what it really meant to follow Jesus? Probably not. Chances are, he knew enough to be honored that the Rabbi from Nazareth—any rabbi, in fact—would call him, an ordinary working man, to become one of his *talmidim*, or disciples.[2] Over time, however, Peter evidently came to understand more thoroughly what he had gotten himself into. He recognized Jesus as "the Messiah, the Son of the living God" (Matthew 16:16). He threw in his lot with Jesus and committed himself so completely that he would say, "Even if all fall away on account of you, I never will" (Matthew 26:33) and "I will lay down my life for you" (John 13:37).

There comes a point in the life of a follower of Jesus when, whether the enthusiasm waxes or wanes, a more definite and determined commitment remains. We surrender more than ever before. We join the church, perhaps, imperfect though it may be. We sign on the dotted line. We pledge our time, talent, and treasure to our Rabbi, our King. We may not slice off anyone's ear with a sword, as Peter did (see John 18:10), but we nonetheless go "all in."

Distraction and Disillusionment

Peter's enthusiasm and commitment were sincere, no doubt. But eventually, reality intruded, as it always does, and he denied he even knew Jesus (see Matthew 26:74–75). Three times, in fact.

Just hours before, Peter was sure he would follow Jesus no matter what. But when "what" came, he faltered and failed. To be fair, the "what" he encountered was a series of events he had not foreseen, could never have anticipated. But that's always the case, isn't it?

Maybe for you it was being overlooked for a hoped-for position. Or sickness set in and healing didn't come. Or Sister Sledgehammer said something hurtful at church. Or it may have been the kids, who found new ways to struggle, even rebel, despite your prayers and best efforts. When "no matter what" runs head-on into a series of events we couldn't have imagined, the result is often distraction, disappointment, and even disillusionment.

Retreat

When Peter denied Jesus, the Bible says that he "wept bitterly" (Matthew 26:75). And days later, even after Jesus rose from the dead and appeared to Peter, among others, the Bible records Peter telling some of his fellow disciples, "I'm going fishing" (John 21:3 NLT). In other words, he went back to what he knew. He didn't set off on his mission. He didn't start preaching in the Temple courts. He went back to his nets where he could find safety, security, insulation. It was the (relatively) easy response.

Similarly, when our enthusiasm wanes and the Christian life gets hard and we feel tired and beat up, we step back—or step out entirely. It's understandable. It's natural, and the (relatively) easy response. But Jesus didn't let Peter get away with that, and, if you're listening to Him at all, He won't let you do so either. Chances are, Jesus will show up even when you're in full retreat.

Spiritual Gut-Check

Sometime after Peter said, "I'm going fishing," Jesus appeared on the shoreline. Maybe it was the same spot where He'd first called out to Peter and his brother, years before. That would make sense. This time, however, Jesus fixed breakfast for Peter and as they ate, He asked Peter three times: "Do you love me?" (see John 21:15–17).

Because that's the point, really.

Not "Did you fall on your face?" Not "Did you deny me?" Not "Was Sister Sledgehammer mean to you? Not "Is it hard to persevere?" or "Is this not what you expected?" It's "Do you love me?" It's not about you, your failures, or even your hurts. Your hurts are real, and they'll need to be dealt with, but the core of what Jesus asks His disciples is, "Do you love me?" That's first and foremost. And if your answer is, like Peter's, "Lord . . . you know that I love you" (John 21:17), then no matter how many times you have to repeat it, you're on the right track, on the threshold of the next part of the journey.

Refreshment and Renewal

Three times Jesus gave Peter a similar message in that breakfast by the sea: "Feed my lambs" (John 21:15), "Take care of my sheep" (John 21:16), "Feed my sheep" (John 21:17). Jesus's call to Peter hadn't changed, through all the enthusiasm, commitment, disillusionment, and even retreat. He just renewed it when Peter was ready.

Notice where Jesus went in His conversation with Peter that day by the sea. He didn't ask about Peter's commitment. He didn't remind Peter of his promises. He didn't say, "Dude, I healed your mother-in-law, remember?" (see Mark 1:29–31). He went straight to the heart and focused on the relationship.

That's the path to refreshment and renewal. Not buckling down, not gritting your teeth, but returning to "the love you had at first" (Revelation 2:4). Then, and only then, will the path forward be clear—and appealing—to you and me.

Empowerment

As far as we know, after his seaside breakfast with Jesus, Peter never went back to fishing. Shortly after, he and his fellow disciples waited in Jerusalem until they received the promised gift of the Holy Spirit—and all the power and blessing he would need for every challenge that was to come (see Acts 2). Years later, having renewed his commitment to Jesus and his flock, Peter would write to other Christ-followers,

> Though you have not seen him, you love him; and even though you do not see him now, you believe in him and are filled with an inexpress-ible and glorious joy. (1 Peter 1:8)

The pathway to an inexpressibly, glorious, joyful relationship with God isn't chucking it all and going fishing; it's found in the answer to Jesus's question: "Do you love me?"

It isn't a distant or elusive possibility, but a "never hungry, never thirsty" reality you can increasingly experience as you draw closer and closer to the heart of God.

Are you ready for that? If so, a prayer like the following may be your next step on that journey:

Lord, you know all things; you know that I love you.

You know, too, that I have sometimes felt empty and discouraged.

You know that I have longed for a different—better—spiritual life.

You know that I want to be closer to you and enjoy the abundant life you promise to your followers.

I believe in you and I am willing to continue reading, hoping, waiting, and learning to be filled with an inexpressible and glorious joy, amen.

CHAPTER TWO

WHO AM I?

She desperately needed access to the king. So much hinged on entering his throne room, drawing closer to him, and laying her requests before him. She prepared herself carefully and strode into his presence, and that changed everything.

You probably know her as Esther, the heroine of the Bible book that bears her name. It's the story of a common young Jewish girl. She was no one important. She lived in Susa, the Persian capital, but Susa wasn't home. She didn't fit in. She had an uncle who loved her, but her father and mother had died. She was an orphan. She was pretty, but she was a woman. She had no rights, fewer privileges, and virtually no prospects. But then one day the king—the absolute ruler of everything and everyone around her—noticed her, accepted her, and exalted her to an honored position.

But that was merely the beginning of the story. At a crucial moment, Esther faced a crisis, and the only one who could solve her problem was the king. So, she went to him. The king heard her request—and answered in dramatic fashion.

Why? How was it that she who had begun life as "Hadassah," a name she shared with the common myrtle bush, could be so close to the king as to receive what she asked? How could she be so brave? How could she enter the king's presence? How could her petitions be answered?

It was because of who she was. She was no longer Hadassah; she was Esther. She was his wife. She could draw near to the king and receive favor. She knew who she was and therefore obtained what she needed.

So it is with you. Esther's story is our story too. Like her, our access and closeness to the King, the absolute Ruler of everything and everyone around us, relies on our understanding and awareness of ourselves, our identity. Are we so much cosmic dust? Carbon molecules? Victims? Losers? Nobodies? As Jean Valjean sings in the *Les Misérables* stage musical: "Who Am I?" Thief? Criminal? Convict? Or redeemed? Righteous? Royalty?

That, as Shakespeare might put it, is the question we all have to answer, particularly if we hope to enjoy a close and thriving relationship with God. How we answer that question can mean the difference between frustration and fulfillment in our spiritual lives.

Who Am I?

What would you say if someone asked you, "Who are you?" How would you answer if that person insisted on a thoughtful, truthful response? What do you truly believe about yourself? Where does your sense of identity come from? Many people would answer in one of the following ways:

Family. As much as we want to think of ourselves as individuals, one of the first and most enduring ways we think of ourselves is as members of a family. Two of Jesus's earliest followers, James and John, were identified (even in adulthood) as "the sons of Zebedee." They were their father's boys (and apparently, from several accounts, their mother's pets). Even if we're an only child, or adopted, or estranged from our family, our sense of identity may come from our family ties—or lack of them.

Appearance. Some people reach adulthood with identities that are largely defined by their appearance: pretty girl, fat kid, too short, too tall, etc. Those labels—even if they exist or endure only in our own minds—can easily come to feel like who we are.

Economic status. Some people answer the question, "Who are you?" in terms of class or money: "poor kid," "trust fund baby," "from the projects," and so on. Sometimes such labels have little to do with external circumstances; a few years ago, I asked my older brothers if they knew they were poor growing up. I was surprised by their answers. "We weren't poor," they said. Strictly speaking, they were right, I guess; we were lower middle class. But I grew up feeling "poor," while they didn't.

Possessions. Some of us define ourselves not by money or class so much as by possessions. A home, maybe, or a car. Season tickets or a musical instrument. We may not be wealthy, but we may still rely on certain possessions to tell us who we are. Maybe that was the situation with the wealthy young man who applied to become one of Jesus's closest followers (see Luke 18:18–27); Jesus loved the man but told him to sell everything and follow Him. The man couldn't do it, perhaps because he couldn't imagine himself apart from his possessions.

Education. Have you ever met someone who quickly mentions her college degree (or degrees) in conversation? Or who makes a point of saying that he "didn't graduate from high school"? Such comments may be a sign of a person whose sense of identity is related to his or her education.

Ethnicity. Some of us think of ourselves partly, even primarily, in ethnic terms. Our identity is wrapped up not only in our family ties but also in race, culture, tradition, and background. Each of these can contribute in healthy ways to our sense of identity, but they can't tell the whole story.

Role. Each of us plays different roles in our lives: child, sibling, parent, employee, teacher, athlete, coach, friend. Some of those roles are so demanding or rewarding that we may come to see a particular role as our primary identity—such as a mother who isn't sure who she is apart from her children, or a business person who feels adrift when not at work.

The past. Among the most common influences we allow to shape our identity is our past: hurts, mistakes, accomplishments, struggles, disappointments, honors. Whether they're haunting or heartening, past experiences often tempt us with their own answers to the question, "Who are you?"

These are far from the only influences that form a sense of identity. But if any of these are primary, we will always struggle to become close to God, to experience a rich and satisfying spiritual life. If, on the other hand, our identity is shaped by something more permanent, something enduring, something transcendent, we will more easily and consistently feel safe, secure, and satisfied in our relationship with God.

Who You Are

Have you ever wondered why Jesus chose to be baptized? His cousin, John the Baptist, did. After all, Jesus hadn't sinned. He had nothing to confess or repent. That's why "John tried to deter him, saying, 'I need to be baptized by you, and do you come to me?'" (Matthew 3:14).

But Jesus insisted. Why?

He told John to humor Him in His effort "to fulfill all righteousness" (Matthew 3:15). There was no Old Testament command He was not obeying, no new command He didn't live up to, so how could His baptism "fulfill all righteousness"? What could it possibly have meant for Him to submit to an act that, for everyone else, symbolized repentance and forgiveness of sins?

I think it was an act of solidarity, a way of saying to John and everyone else—including us today—"I am one of you. I throw in my lot with you. I'm not separate. I'm not aloof. I identify with you. I align myself with the whole, messy, sinful lot of you." He identified with us in every way so that we may identify with Him in every way, which is part of the symbolism when we are baptized as followers of Jesus. We become new creations (see 2 Corinthians 5:17) with new identities. Whatever we were before, we are no longer; we "were therefore buried with him through baptism into death in order that, just as Christ was raised from the dead through the glory of the Father, we too may live a new life" (Romans 6:4). Our identity isn't who we say we are or what others think we are, but all that God has re-created us to be through Jesus Christ:

a masterpiece, not a mistake (Ephesians 2:10)

accepted, not rejected (Romans 15:7)

forgiven, not forgotten (Colossians 2:13)

righteous, not guilty (2 Corinthians 5:21)

clean and confident, not ashamed (1 Corinthians 6:11, Hebrews 10:22)

begraced, not begrudged (Hebrews 4:16)

sons and daughters, not orphans (Romans 8:15, 1 John 3:1)

heirs, not paupers (Romans 8:17)

privileged, not outcast (1 Peter 2:9)

whole, not broken (Colossians 2:10)

partners with God, not purposeless (1 Corinthians 3:9)

close to God, not distant (Ephesians 2:13, Hebrews 10:22).

Whatever identities we have accepted or assumed for ourselves, the traits above are what we now enjoy through the grace of God and kindness of our Savior, Jesus Christ. He has made us anew and given us identities that no longer rely on temporary roles or fleeting characteristics, but rather foster an intimate and enduring connection with God. Like Queen Esther of Persia, whose conferred identity gave her the privilege and blessing of access to the king (see Esther 5), our identities as followers of Jesus grant us admittance into God's presence and the blessing of a closer relationship with Him than we have ever previously known.

Is it a struggle to see yourself the way God sees you?

If so, it'll be difficult for you to draw as close to God as you want to—and as He wants you to. But if you can begin to grasp your true identity in Christ, you'll open the door to the very throne room of God and stride toward a new and closer relationship with Him. One way to move in that direction is to sincerely and thoughtfully pray a prayer like the following:

Lord God, my King,
  please open my eyes so that I may see you more clearly,
  and see myself more and more as you see me.
  Help me to believe and accept the truth of who you say I am,
  rather than listening to the lies I have believed in the past.
  I choose to believe that I am a new creation.
  I choose to believe that I am a masterpiece, not a mistake.
  I choose to believe that I am freely and fully accepted by you, not rejected.
  I choose to believe that I am forgiven, not forgotten.
  I choose to believe that in Christ I am righteous, not guilty.
  I choose to believe that I am clean and confident, not ashamed.
  I choose to believe that I am begraced, not begrudged.

I choose to believe that I am a child of God, not an orphan.

I choose to believe that I am an heir, not a pauper.

I choose to believe that I am privileged, not outcast, part of a chosen people, a royal priesthood, a holy nation, a special family that belongs to God.

I choose to believe that I am whole, not broken.

I choose to believe that I am your partner in your great mission, not purposeless.

I choose to believe that I who once was far from you have been brought near by the blood of Jesus Christ, in whose name I pray, amen.

CHAPTER THREE

CAN'T GET THERE . . .

You can't get there from here."

Have you ever asked for directions and heard those words? It seems ridiculous, because you just need directions to get where you want to go. Surely there is a way to get there, right?

But the phrase suggests that there is something in your way. There is no direct route to where you want to go. You have to regroup, rethink, or retrace your steps in order to get to your destination.

That's sometimes how it is in our quest to be closer to God. We may be frustrated because we can't get there from where we are. Something is in our way. We have to regroup, rethink, or retrace our steps to see if our forward progress is stymied by assumptions and pressures that hinder us in our relationships with God.

Early in His earthly ministry, Jesus made a series of statements that surprised His listeners because they overturned many of their traditions and assumptions about the godly life and the way the world works. He went up on a hillside and sat down. His closest followers accompanied Him, and a crowd gathered. Jesus began to teach them:

> Blessed are the poor in spirit,
>   for theirs is the kingdom of heaven.
> Blessed are those who mourn,
>   for they will be comforted.
> Blessed are the meek,
>   for they will inherit the earth.
> Blessed are those who hunger and thirst for
>   righteousness,
>   for they will be filled.
> Blessed are the merciful,
>   for they will be shown mercy.
> Blessed are the pure in heart,
>   for they will see God.
> Blessed are the peacemakers,
>   for they will be called children of God.
> Blessed are those who are persecuted be-
>   cause of righteousness,
>   for theirs is the kingdom of heaven.

Then He apparently turned His gaze on His close friends and devoted followers and addressed them: "Blessed are you when people insult you, persecute you and falsely say all kinds of evil against you because of me. Rejoice and be glad, because great is your reward in heaven, for in the same way they persecuted the prophets who were before you" (Matthew 5:1–12).

Beautiful words, right? But they're easily misunderstood. First, it helps to understand that when we read the word "blessed" in our Bibles, we're looking at a translation of a Greek word which means "happy." But it means something different from the circumstantial "feel-goodism" that we associate with the English word; Jesus was talking about a deep, abiding, joyful kind of happiness. And it's also different from what Jesus's first listeners expected.

Many of us read, "Blessed are the poor in spirit," and "Blessed are those who mourn," and think, "Hmm. I guess I should try to be like that." But that wasn't Jesus's point at all. He wasn't prescribing states we should try to achieve; He was holding out hope and breaking down barriers that kept people from drawing near to God.

Jesus said, in effect, "You know what? You guys think happiness is only for the rich and religiously connected. But I'm here to tell you, even 'the spiritual zeroes'[1] should be happy because the kingdom of heaven belongs to them as much as it does to anyone.

"You think only those who are riding high have reason to be happy, but I'm telling you that those who mourn should be happy, because they will be comforted, as the prophet Isaiah promised (see Isaiah 40:1–3).

"You think you have to be assertive and powerful to be happy? No! I'm telling you that even the meek and lowly are my heirs. You think because you feel spiritually empty that you're hopeless? I'm saying you should be happy because you're in the right place for a spiritual outpouring and infilling. You think the cruelty and oppression you see all around you means God is on the side of your oppressors? No, I'm telling you the merciful will receive mercy from God. You see wickedness and war making people rich and happy? Don't be silly. I'm telling you the pure in heart and those who make peace will be the richest and happiest of all. And you think that persecution means your Father has forgotten you? I'm saying be happy because your Father has better things in store for you than you even know."

The good news that Jesus proclaimed on that hillside dispelled many of their misgivings and misconceptions that were holding them back, keeping them distant from God, and preventing them from experiencing the rich relationships with God that they craved. He was saying in effect, "you can't get where you want to go from where you are. So, let's erase some of your stinkin' thinkin' and pave the way for the life you long for."

What if their need is also our need? What if we struggle to enjoy a closer relationship with God because of some stubborn assumptions? Could our own stinkin' thinkin' hinder us from flourishing spiritually?

A Few New Beatitudes

"Blessed are those who don't have their acts together."

We may know that we don't have to get our act together in order to follow Christ (after all, we come to Him in the first place because we need forgiveness, cleansing, and a new start). But many of us think that once we've experienced new life in Christ, we're supposed to figure things out pretty quickly. We should more or less straighten up and fly right from the start. And if we don't, well, then there's something wrong with us and we suspect God may be displeased with us. But even a cursory look at the first followers of Jesus—who consistently struggled with hotheadedness, bigotry, doubt, and more—will show the truth of Brennan Manning's words:

> The Kingdom . . . is not a subdivision for the self-righteous nor for those who feel they possess the state secret of their salvation. The Kingdom is not an exclusive, well-trimmed suburb with snobbish rules about who can live there. No, it's a far larger, homelier, less self-conscious cast of people who understand they are sinners because they have experienced the yaw and pitch of moral struggle.[2]

So be happy if you don't feel as if you have your act together yet, for God is pleased to help you grow and "mature in the Lord, measuring up to the full and complete standard of Christ" (Ephesians 4:13 NLT).

"Blessed are those whose spiritual lives aren't a smooth, ever upward trajectory."

Have you ever walked on a glacier? My cousin George and his wife Jeanne took me and my wife, the lovely Robin, to the Matanuska Glacier in Alaska a few years ago. George explained that even though the surface under our feet looked like asphalt, it was actually ice, and we needed to step carefully as we ascended farther up the glacier's surface. All went well, and none of us slipped, until George fell hard on a downward slope. If the walk had been a smooth, upward journey—both ways—it might have been different, but we didn't tease George for being the only one who took a tumble. Much.

Similarly, sometimes we stumble in our efforts to pursue and enjoy a close relationship with God because we don't expect any dips or detours. We feel deflated or defeated if we experience anything short of smooth sailing and steady progress. We aren't so different from Peter, who boldly confessed Jesus as "the Christ, the Son of the living God." That earned him heady praise from Jesus himself: "Blessed are you, Simon Bar-Jonah!" Moments after, Peter responded to Jesus's warnings about His coming death by saying, "Far be it from you, Lord!" which prompted Jesus to say, "Get behind me, Satan!" (Matthew 16:16–17, 22–23 ESV).

That had to sting, but it shows that we're not the first or the only ones whose spiritual lives have multiple ups and downs. It also shows that we can be happy if our spiritual life isn't a smooth, ever upward trajectory, because those hills and valleys, twists and turns, can draw us closer to God, if we let them, making us moment-by-moment more "mature and complete, not lacking anything" (James 1:4).

"Blessed are those whose spiritual lives don't look like someone else's spiritual life."

All of us learn from others, and that's a good thing. We admire people whose faith inspires us. We want to emulate those whose faces seem to shine with the glory and grace of God. But the godliness of others can also leave us wondering: Why does my relationship with Jesus seem so different? Why can't my "walk with God" be more like my pastor's? Or friends'? Or teacher's? Why can't I pray like her? Why can't I memorize Scripture like him? What is *wrong* with me?

But again, look at those earliest followers of Jesus. Were they all alike? Did they all have helicopter moms like James and John? Did they all contradict Jesus like Peter? Did they all demand proof like Thomas? Of course not. They were individuals, and so are you. Your prayer life doesn't have to look like your pastor's. Your path in growing closer to God doesn't have to track with your cousin's. So be happy that your spiritual life doesn't look like anyone else's, because your destiny isn't to become more and more like them, but more and more like Jesus (2 Corinthians 3:18).

These are just a few new beatitudes. They don't come close to the beauty and inspiration of Jesus's words from the Sermon on the Mount. And there may be other assumptions and misconceptions that are holding you back and preventing you from drawing closer to God. If that's the case, take a few moments to search your heart and consider what you believe—or suspect—about you and God, and your relationship with Him. Ask Him to reveal to you anything that might be standing in the way of you growing closer to Him. And, whatever He reveals, ask for Him to open the door to greater wisdom and understanding so that you can enjoy a new and growing closeness to Him. That's a prayer He loves to answer, so why not start now by praying something like,

---

Lord Jesus, thank you that I don't have my act together, that I haven't yet figured everything out, because I believe that you are pleased to help me grow and mature day by day until I measure up "to the full and complete standard of Christ" (Ephesians 4:13 NLT).

Thank you that my spiritual life is full of ups and downs instead of a smooth, ever upward trajectory, because I believe that those hills and valleys, twists and turns, are drawing me ever closer to you and making me more and more "mature and complete, not lacking anything" (James 1:4).

And thank you that my spiritual life doesn't look like anyone else's (even those people I envy or admire), because I believe that my destiny isn't to become more like them, but to be transformed more and more like Jesus (2 Corinthians 3:18).

Please reveal to me anything that's standing in the way of a closer relationship to you.

Please open the door of my heart and mind to greater wisdom and understanding so that I can enjoy a new and growing closeness to you, amen.

CHAPTER FOUR

BUMPER CAR FAITH

My spiritual life feels like a carnival ride."

My friend Lisa's comment made me smile. "Like how? Fun? Thrilling? Scary?"

She shook her head. "No. More like the bumper cars."

"How do you mean?"

She shrugged, and for a moment I thought she might drop the subject. But she didn't. Her explanation went something like this, "I'm sure there's power coming from above—like the current that runs down the pole to the bumper cars—but no matter which way I turn I hit an obstacle. I want more of God, but I feel like I can never get where

I want to go. I'm constantly frustrated. Sometimes I even get turned around and end up going backwards."

I was impressed. The life of faith does feel that way at times.

It seems as though the pursuit of a closer relationship with God ought to be easier than it is. Surely the trouble isn't with God, or His willingness to draw near to us. He says, "Come to me, all you who are weary and burdened" and "Whoever comes to me I will never drive away" (Matthew 11:28, John 6:37).

He's always willing to draw near to us, so why do we have such difficulty getting closer to Him? What are the obstacles in our way? What frustrates us in our quest to experience a closer, thriving, rewarding relationship with God?

A Heavy Load

The other women in the village had all come and gone from the well before she balanced a clay jar on her head and headed out. The sun stood high in the sky and the path ahead shimmered from the heat. She didn't mind. The late hour and the scorching sun meant she was unlikely to cross paths with anyone else. It was better that way. She knew they despised her, and she'd rather just finish her errand and return to the hovel she shared with her new boyfriend.

But as she approached, she saw a man sitting in the shade beside the well. She saw he was a Jew, and knew he wouldn't speak to her. Probably wouldn't even look at her. In fact, he might get up and hurry away so as not to be contaminated by contact with a Samaritan woman.

But he didn't leave. He spoke. He asked her for a drink.

She lowered her jar to the ground. "You—you are a Jew and I am a Samaritan woman. How can you ask me for a drink?"

The man's voice was gentle—not at all what she expected. "If you knew the gift of God and who it is that asks you for a drink, you would ask him." He smiled. "And he would have given you living water."

She inspected the ground around where he sat. "Sir, you have nothing to draw with and the well is deep. Where can you get this living water? Are you greater than our father Jacob, who gave us the well and drank from it himself, as did also his sons and his livestock?"

"Everyone who drinks this water will be thirsty again, but whoever drinks the water I give them will never thirst. Indeed, the water I give them will become in them a spring of water welling up to eternal life."

"Sir, give me this water."

He told her to go and get her husband and come back. She lowered her gaze to the dust at her feet. "I have no husband."

"Yes, I know. You have had five husbands, and the man you now have is not your husband."

She covered her mouth with her hand. Who was this man? How did he know? How could he see so far into her guilty heart? He was a Jewish man, and yet he talked to her, a strange woman. She was a Samaritan, and yet he smiled at her. More than that, he knew her story—her past, her sin, her guilt—and he didn't turn away. He didn't shake his head or cluck his tongue.

What a moment that must have been for that Samaritan woman!

When the man—Jesus of Nazareth, she learned later—revealed himself as the long-awaited Messiah, she did the unthinkable. Moments before, she'd felt too burdened with guilt to join the other women as they fetched the daily water in the morning and so came in the heat of the day instead. Now she ran into the village, called at gates and knocked on doors to tell all of the people who despised her that she'd just met "the Savior of the world" (John 4:42).

Guilt does awful things to us. It hinders our relationships, not only with others but also with God himself. If we suspect Jesus is displeased, our feelings may prevent us from drawing close to God, no matter how much we may long for His presence.

If, like the woman at the well, we're carrying the heavy load of true guilt—the result of a sin we've committed and the conviction of the Holy Spirit in the heart—there is a solution: "If we confess our sins, he is faithful and just and will forgive us our sins and purify us from all unrighteousness" (1 John 1:9). True guilt says, "I sinned," and the remedy for it is to confess the sin and accept God's forgiveness and cleansing.

However, if we can't identify any sin that's preventing us from drawing near to God, we may be feeling false guilt. False guilt isn't the result of sin. It may come from regret ("I wish things had been different"), insecurity ("Why do I always say the wrong thing?"), or even obsession ("I know it was fifteen years ago, but I can't believe I wore that"). Though it isn't true guilt, it sure can *feel* like guilt. And false guilt can produce feelings of condemnation, a sense that God is often (or always) upset with us, in turn prompting dissatisfaction, depression, and a spiritual paralysis. False guilt must be recognized and resisted—as often and consistently as necessary—with the truth that "there is now no condemnation for those who are in Christ Jesus" (Romans 8:1).

The Dark Corner

Twelve years she'd suffered from a humiliating and repulsive condition. She'd tried everything the doctors and rabbis thought might work. She'd sat at a crossroads, holding a cup of wine until a man snuck up from behind to startle her and exclaim, "Cease your discharge!" She'd rubbed various foul-smelling mixtures on her body. She'd spent three days clutching a barleycorn that had been found in the dung of a white mule. But nothing had worked. She'd spent all she had, and her condition had only worsened.

Then she heard that the Rabbi from Nazareth was healing everyone who came to Him. But there was a problem. Her condition made her unclean. Anyone who touched her would instantly also become unclean. Anyone she touched would be unclean.

But maybe there was a way . . .

She traveled on foot to find Jesus, and when she finally saw Him, her heart fell. He was surrounded by swarms of people. Could she really enter that crowd? What if someone recognized her? What if her menstrual stench ruined everything before she reached Him? She almost turned back. But some people were saying He was the Messiah. She knew the promise God gave through the prophet: "But for you who fear my name, the Sun of Righteousness will rise with healing in his wings" (Malachi 4:2 NLT). She knew the word "wings" could refer to a man's *tzitzit*, the fringed or tasseled corners of his *tallit*, his prayer shawl.[1] She reasoned, "If I can only touch that tassel, I will be healed." She believed. She had to. She was desperate. She'd lived as an outcast, in sickness and shame, for much too long.

So, she lowered her head and stole forward, trying to be inconspicuous, cringing every time someone jostled her, but determined to just . . . reach . . . Him. Her fingers found one tasseled corner and she felt an immediate change in her body. She let go.

And then the Nazarene stopped.

The crowd halted.

She froze.

Jesus turned. "Who touched my clothes?"

Oh no. She shrank.

His followers protested and pointed to the throng surrounding Him. But Jesus kept turning until His gaze settled on her. She'd planned to slip away quietly, without anyone knowing about what she'd done. But He'd found her out. She lurched forward and fell to the ground at his feet, trembling. Somehow, between sobs, she confessed everything—her past, her shame, her desperation.

He stooped and touched her. He *touched* her. And said, "Daughter, your faith has healed you. Go in peace and be freed from your suffering" (Mark 5:34).

Imagine that woman as she returned home that day. She probably laughed and leapt and sang as she went home. Do you think she may also have reflected on how close she came to letting shame keep her away? Did she tremble at the thought of almost missing the Healer's touch? How sad it would have been if shame had kept her from pressing close to Jesus, receiving healing and hearing Him say, "your faith has healed you. Go in peace and be freed from your suffering."

Whatever affliction or status makes you feel unclean, no matter where you live or what you do, whoever else may despise you or scorn you, He does not. You may feel broken and bruised, but "A bruised reed he will not break" (Isaiah 42:3). You may feel all used up and all burnt out, but "a smoldering wick he will not snuff out" (Isaiah 42:3). Whatever you've done, whatever your past, whatever you've suffered, whatever you regret, let Jesus heal your shame at its source.

Would you stay away from the doctor because you had a fever? Or avoid the grocery store because you were hungry? Of course not. Why would you let any sense of shame keep you from drawing closer to the One who heals body and soul? Christ wasn't repulsed by the leper; He didn't turn away any demoniacs. He even called a despised, traitorous tax collector to follow Him.

And to the woman who'd been unclean for twelve years, he said, "your faith has healed you. Go in peace and be freed from your suffering" (Mark 5:34). A touch from Him can remove your shame too, and the closer you get to Him, the closer you are to healing, peace, and freedom.

Shaky Ground

Nothing hurts more than watching your child suffer.

That's why the man left home with his son. Together they went looking for Jesus, and when they finally joined the crowds that'd been traveling the countryside with the rabbi from Nazareth, they learned that Jesus had gone up into the mountain overlooking the plain with a few of His closest followers.

Undeterred, the man pleaded with the disciples who awaited Jesus's return. He explained that his son was possessed by a spirit that had left him unable to speak. The spirit would seize the boy and throw him to the ground, foaming at the mouth and gnashing his teeth.

So one of Jesus's disciples laid his hands on the boy and commanded the demon to come out. Nothing happened. Another tried, and still nothing.

The man's heart sank, until he saw several men coming down from the mountain. Surely one of them was Jesus. He ran to them, and quickly identified the Rabbi. He explained what had happened.

"You unbelieving generation," Jesus replied, "how long shall I stay with you? How long shall I put up with you?"

The father clasped his hands together to beg, afraid that Jesus's words were directed at him. But Jesus's next words filled him with hope.

"Bring the boy to me."

The man dashed to his son's side and ran back to where Jesus stood, waiting. Immediately the demon-possessed boy dropped to the ground in a convulsion. He writhed and foamed at the mouth. It was terrifying. The father fell to his knees beside the boy, tears streaming down his face.

"How long has he been like this?" Jesus asked.

He looked up at Jesus while his boy still screamed and struggled. "From childhood. It has often thrown him into fire or water to kill him." He shook his head. "But if you can do anything, take pity on us and help us."

"'If you can'?"

Did Jesus smile just then?

"Everything is possible for one who believes."

The boy's father jumped to his feet. He leaned closer to Jesus. "I do believe; help me overcome my unbelief!"

Jesus looked around. The crowd was growing. He spoke without raising His voice. "You deaf and mute spirit, I command you, come out of him and never enter him again."

A shriek split the air, and the boy's form convulsed violently before going limp. Jesus reached down, took his hand, and lifted him to his feet—and in his right mind.[2]

The boy's father begged Jesus, "If you can do anything, take pity on us and help us."

Don't you love Jesus's response to the despairing father?

"If you can?"

It almost feels like a friendly taunt, doesn't it? Did that man know to whom he was speaking? Maybe not. He may only have heard there was a healer in the neighborhood. His health insurance company may have said Jesus was the only in-network provider in the area. We don't know. But when Jesus said, "Everything is possible for one who believes," the father answered, "I do believe; help me overcome my unbelief!" (Mark 9:23–24).

He didn't say, "What're you talking about, Jesus? Of course I believe!"

He didn't say, "Okay, okay, I really, really believe."

He didn't say, "I think I can, I think I can."

He acknowledged that he believed . . . some. But he made himself transparent before God, admitting that he still had doubts. That's healthy. That's honest. That's more than you and I sometimes are willing to do.

Look, it's normal that doubts can occasionally get in the way of our relationships with God. Doubts may make us feel guilty or ashamed. Doubts may cause us to neglect prayer, wondering if it really does any good. Doubts can prompt us to be spiritually lazy, sapping our motivation and energy for the actions that would draw us closer to God. Doubts can be particularly harmful to our spiritual lives if we lie about them to ourselves and to God.

But doubt can also be healthy, particularly if we confront and confess our doubts, praying the prayer of the boy's father: "I do believe; help me overcome my unbelief!" Doubt can drive us to think things through and study more deeply. Doubt can actually end up enlarging and enhancing our faith; as we become more and more honest with God, we become more intimate with Him as well.

Whatever barrier or obstacle you face in your relationship with God—and it may be something besides guilt, shame, or doubt—why not take a few minutes now to pray about that obstacle? You might pray one or all of the following:

Lord, I confess that I have sinned against you, through my own fault, in what I have done and in what I have left undone; thank you for your mercy and grace in forgiving my sin and cleansing me from all unrighteousness by the sacrificial work of Jesus on my behalf. Help me to live every day in the awareness that I am forgiven, clean, and free of condemnation.

Jesus, I reach out to you for healing from shame. Please grant me peace and freedom from suffering, and remind me moment-by-moment that I have been touched, accepted, and healed by you. Remind me constantly of who you are, who I am, and whose I am.

God, increase my faith. Change my "If you can" to "I believe; help me overcome my un-belief." Deliver me from any doubts that get in the way of my relationship with you, and help me to believe that expressing my desire to draw near to you is already drawing us closer and closer together, in Jesus's name, amen.

CHAPTER FIVE

THOSE GUYS HAD IT MADE

We think that Jesus's earliest followers had it made.

Don't you? I often do. After all, those people actually met Him in the flesh, walked beside Him. The Twelve often slept on the ground next to Him. They heard Him speak, saw Him heal, helped Him distribute miracle food to thousands, ran errands for Him, and even watched Him raise the dead. They were as close to Him as anyone could be, and anyone who was close to Him was close to the Father also. Wouldn't it be great to do as they did? To be as close to the Incarnate God as they were?

Wouldn't it be great to be able to cry out to Jesus in panicked moments? When a storm at sea threatened to swamp their boat while Jesus was sleeping, they woke Him and said, "Lord, save us! We're going to drown!" And He did. When Peter walked on water, until he didn't, and then he cried out, "Lord, save me!" And He did.

Wouldn't it be great to be able to ask Christ questions any time we wanted? Like when John the Baptist's disciples asked Jesus, "How come the Pharisees fast, and we fast—often, in fact—but your followers don't fast?" Or when a fig tree withered after Jesus cursed it for not bearing fruit, and the disciples asked, basically, "Wha—? How?" Or when Jesus told a memorable parable and later they pulled Him aside and asked Him, "What did it all mean?"

How sweet would it be to have the ability to suggest our ideas and actions to Jesus? Like when some of His followers said, "This is a pretty remote place, and it's getting kind of late. So shouldn't you stop talking and send the crowds away, so they can get some dinner?" Or when Peter got so excited after seeing Jesus talking on a mountaintop with Moses and Elijah that he said something like, "Here's an idea. Let me build three shelters here—one each for you, Moses, and Elijah. Whaddya say?"

It would also be great if we could complain to Jesus anytime we felt like it, as His first followers did, seemingly all the time. Like when John the son of Zebedee came to Him and reported (without mentioning any names, mind you) that they had seen someone driving out demons in Jesus's name "and we told him to stop, because he was not one of us" (Mark 9:38). Or when some in Jesus's entourage complained that some of His teachings were a bit extreme (see John 6:60).

Those early followers of Jesus had the advantage of being able to ask for special favors (Luke 4:38, Mark 10:35), prod Him for compliments (Matthew 18:1, 21), lodge protests (Matthew 19:25, 26:8–9), express regret (John 11:21), register amazement (Matthew 21:20), and pledge their loyalty (Mark 14:29, 31). They even felt close enough to Him and open enough with Him to occasionally rebuke Him (see Matthew 16:22, Mark 4:38).

All of those things reflect a closeness and comfort that we can only imagine and envy. Right?

Wrong.

Every one of those signs of intimacy with Jesus is available to us—more so, in fact, because those first followers had to wait for an opportunity, when the crowds weren't pressing in on Jesus for example, or when Moses and Elijah found someplace else to be.

They had to wait to ask questions or request favors when they returned from, say, borrowing a donkey or reserving a banquet room. They had to wait for Jesus to wake up or come down from the mountain where He went to pray. Sure, maybe they had the advantage of seeing Him in the flesh, but we have the advantage of drawing close to Jesus instantly, constantly, anywhere and everywhere . . . through prayer.

Open the Door

If you're anything like me, your interest level dropped when I mentioned prayer—at least like me as I was for many years, even as a pastor. Prayer is boring, we think sometimes. Tedious. A monologue and not a dialogue. Necessary, maybe, but definitely not fun or interesting. But I think those hidden perceptions are because of how we've learned prayer and tried to practice it, not because of what it really is. We've made it into something it's not.

Our idea of the praying person may be of someone sitting with a Bible in his lap, praying from 4 a.m. until breakfast. Or that of a gray-haired woman folding her hands over a plate of food. Or a child kneeling at his bedside. And those are all fine images of prayer—but they may be counterproductive for many people and might even have seemed strange to those first followers of Jesus. Why? Because they simply kept company with Jesus. They ate and drank with Him, and asked Him questions, and sometimes even argued with Him. Their life-changing, even world-changing closeness to God was a product of their proximity to Jesus.

Why can't it be that way for us? Something more like what those first followers of Jesus experienced? In fact, I think that reality is implicit in an oft-misunderstood verse of the Bible, one many church-goers have heard often and Bible readers have read repeatedly. But we may never have heard it the way Jesus intended.

The last book of the Bible, Revelation, quotes Jesus as saying, "Here I am! I stand at the door and knock. If anyone hears my voice and opens the door, I will come in and eat with that person, and they with me" (Revelation 3:20). Many Bible preachers, teachers, readers, and students have understood those words as a beautiful verse about opening your heart to Jesus and becoming "born again." But that's not what that verse is about.

Revelation 3:20 is part of a letter which the risen Jesus dictated to John, His disciple, who relayed it to a church in a town called Laodicea. It wasn't written to pagans, unbelievers, or seekers. It wasn't written to people attending an evangelistic service or responding to an altar call. It was written to specific people in a specific church who were being urged to repent and turn from their lukewarm ways. Jesus said to them, in effect, "Hey, open up. I want to come in. I want to eat with you. I want to keep company with you."

That's what Zacchaeus heard and understood when Jesus said (my paraphrase), "Dude, come out of that tree. I want to come to your house. I want to eat with you. I would like to keep company with Zacchaeus the tax-collector." And Jesus wants to keep company with us, too. He invites us into an ongoing conversation that includes not only our heartfelt confessions and requests but also our panic, our questions, our suggestions, affirmations, protests, and regrets. He doesn't even mind an occasional rebuke or honest argument (provided we're prepared to hear "get behind me, Satan," in reply).

That's what prayer is. That's what it should be, anyway. That's what Jesus longs for, with you and me. He doesn't frown on "God is great, God is good," but it must break His heart if the conversation ends there. He wants to come in and eat with us, through the whole meal, and afterward too.

Can you imagine if His first followers had thanked Jesus for their breakfast by the Sea of Galilee and then turned to each other and ignored Him for the rest of the meal? Christ's Holy Spirit is present with us just as He was with James, John, and Peter, and He is attentive, listening, and speaking not only to "Bless us, O Lord, and these thy gifts" and "Now I lay me down to sleep," but in every moment in between.

Philip Yancey, in his book titled simply *Prayer*, wrote:

I am writing away from home, sequestered in the mountains in the middle of winter. At the end of each day I talk with my wife, Janet, about the events of the day. I tell her how many words I wrote and what obstacles I met in the process, what Nordic ski or snowshoe trails I explored . . . which prepackaged frozen foods I ate for dinner. She tells me about the progress of her nagging cold, the mail that has been accumulating in my absence, the neighbors she has encountered walking their dogs to the mailboxes down the road. We discuss the weather, current events, news from relatives, upcoming social engagements. In essence, we meditate on the day with each other, in the process bringing the details into a new light.

What I have just described bears a striking resemblance to prayer, too. Prayer, according to one ancient definition, is 'keeping company with God.'[1]

I believe that's not only what God wants from each one of us and for each one of us, but I also think that's a missing ingredient in many of our spiritual lives. Our focus is often on saying prayers, when Jesus wants us to simply keep company with him. Every day. Throughout the day. When we're otherwise alone and when we're with others.

Pray a New Way

Does that seem "easier said than done?" Maybe. But for some people, keeping company with Jesus is refreshingly and rejuvenatingly different from the burdensome ways they've tried to draw closer to God in the past. Maybe it can begin for you with some or all of these ideas:

Ask for the ability to pray a new way. That's exactly what Jesus's first followers and closest friends did. When they came to Jesus and asked, "Lord, teach us to pray" (Luke 11:1), they weren't newcomers to prayer. They were Jews; they'd prayed all their lives, every day, every morning, every meal. But they asked Jesus to show them a new way to pray. We can do the same, and as with any spiritual blessing in our lives, the blessing of a new way to pray begins with prayer.

Pray without guilt or comparison. So much frustration in prayer comes from trying to pray like someone else, whether it's the prophet Daniel, who knelt to pray three times every day, or Martin Luther, who famously said, "I have so much to do that I shall spend the first three hours in prayer,"[2] or the missionary John Nelson Hyde ("Praying Hyde"), who would often spend entire nights in prayer.[3] If such examples inspire you and work for you, great! But if they don't, determine not to let guilt or comparison drive your efforts to get closer to God. Instead, grant yourself the grace and freedom to explore and experiment, which can infuse your journey with joy and anticipation.

Pray without pretense. In His famous "Sermon on the Mount," Jesus said,

> When you pray, do not be like the hypocrites, for they love to pray standing in the synagogues and on the street corners to be seen by others. Truly I tell you, they have received their reward in full. But when you pray, go into your room, close the door and pray to your

Father, who is unseen. Then your Father, who sees what is done in secret, will reward you. And when you pray, do not keep on babbling like pagans, for they think they will be heard because of their many words. Do not be like them, for your Father knows what you need before you ask him. (Matthew 6:5–8)

We don't have to say "Thee" and "Thou" when we pray. We don't have to quote the Bible or use big words. We don't need to impress God . . . or anyone else. Like the picture of prayer that Jesus painted, we can pray simply, humbly, and plainly.

Pray honestly. We won't draw closer to God until we're honest with Him, until we tell Him exactly and completely what's in our hearts and minds— and not just what we think He wants to hear. He already knows what's inside us, so it makes no sense to tell Him anything less than the plain, unvarnished truth—like Martha saying to Jesus, "if you had been here, my brother would not have died" (John 11:21) or the Twelve crying out in the midst of a storm, "don't you care if we drown?" (Mark 4:38).

Look for ways to pray throughout the day. Keeping company with Jesus may start with a habit of saying, "Good morning, Lord," as you tumble out of bed. Or listening to a worship song or prayer podcast as you brush your teeth at night. Or, when you hear a siren, praying for the urgent need it announces, and the people who race to meet it. Or when you open a card or email from a friend, asking Jesus to bless the sender.

"Here I am!" Jesus says. "I stand at the door and knock. If anyone hears my voice and opens the door, I will come in and eat with that person, and they with me" (Revelation 3:20). It's not an invitation to a discipline, much less a duty or drudgery. It's an offer to carry on an ongoing conversation, as you would with the dearest of friends, one who is always present, and never leaves you.

Lord, teach me to pray. Show me how to pray a new way, to open the door wide and keep company with you, to engage in an ongoing conversation with you that includes not only heartfelt confessions and requests but also my panic, questions, suggestions, affirmations, protests, and regrets —and every moment and emotion in between. Help me to pray without guilt or comparison, without pretense, with complete honesty. Remind me to pray throughout the day, every day, when the two of us are otherwise alone and when we're with others, that I might know you and draw closer to you, the dearest of friends, amen.

CHAPTER SIX

EARS TO HEAR

I couldn't wait for her to stop talking.

Don't get me wrong. My first date with the woman who is now my wife was wonderful in every way. Ours was a summer camp romance, so we walked to the campfire circle and then sat beneath a canopy of trees while she talked. And talked. And talked.

I listened. Or at least pretended to listen. But I spent most of that blissful evening waiting for a pause in the conversation—or monologue—so that I could sneak in a kiss. It finally happened. She reached the end of a sentence and I punctuated it with a short kiss.

She saw through me. "You've just been waiting for me to stop talking, haven't you?"

I admitted it, and she kissed me back.

That wasn't the last time that I failed to listen closely to what she said, but we've been together forty-plus years since then. I've learned to listen much better, even as I've snuck more than a few kisses. True, the lovely Robin (as I am wont to call her) feels comfortable speaking many more words each day than I do, but we both speak and we both listen. That's what it takes to develop a good, healthy, and lasting relationship.

If you really want to know someone—if you long to grow closer and more intimate with anyone—you don't just talk. You listen, too. A relationship with God through Jesus Christ is no different. "My sheep listen to my voice," Jesus said (John 10:27). Of course, we tend to do most or all of the talking in our relationship with God, which may be partly why we struggle to feel closer to Him. Close relationships are two-way streets; they're fueled by roughly equal parts give and take, talking and listening. We get to know God better, and draw closer to Him, as we learn not only to talk to Him but also to listen to Him.

Listen to His Words

Why do we read the Bible—have you ever asked that question? Maybe not, because we just know we're supposed to. It's an important part of the Christian life, right? But why? Do we read it for entertainment, as a person might read a novel? Do we read it as an escape, a way to leave the world behind, the way some people enjoy a good "beach read"? Do we read it for information? Instruction? Inspiration? All of the above?

The Bible can be read in all of those ways. Parts of it are entertaining, even funny (Balaam's donkey in Numbers 22:21–39 comes to mind). It can provide an escape for someone who wants to get lost in a good story (the book of Jonah) or swept up in a beautiful poem (Song of Songs). Much of it is chock full of information, as well as instruction, and certainly inspiration. But the Bible wasn't given to you primarily for those reasons. Here's what I mean.

Imagine you were in the room that Sabbath day in Nazareth when Jesus read from the Isaiah scroll. We don't know if any of His followers were there, but we can imagine what it might've been like if you and I were watching, listening.

We see Jesus step up onto the *bimah*, the raised platform, and take the scroll from the *gabbai*, the synagogue official who calls the readers forward.[1]

We wait while Jesus unrolls the scroll and begins to read:

The Spirit of the Lord is on me,
because he has anointed me
to proclaim good news to the poor.
He has sent me to proclaim freedom for
the prisoners
and recovery of sight for the blind,
to set the oppressed free,
to proclaim the year of the Lord's favor.
(Luke 4:18–19)

We watch in silence as Jesus rolls up the scroll, gives it back to the *gabbai*, sits down and says, "Today this scripture is fulfilled in your hearing."

With those words, something changes. Jesus has done something momentous. He hasn't given the reading for instruction or inspiration, primarily. He applied the words to himself. He started a conversation.

What would you have said to Jesus at that moment? If you and He had been the only ones in the room? How would you have responded? How do you imagine the conversation proceeding?

That's what it means to read the Bible, not out of obligation or habit, but relationally. It's one of the ways of listening to Jesus and carrying on a conversation with Him. That's why Jesus told the religious leaders of His day, "You have your heads in your Bibles constantly because you think you'll find eternal life there. But you miss the forest for the trees. These Scriptures are all about me! And here I am, standing right before you, and you aren't willing to receive from me the life you say you want" (John 5:39–40 MSG). The best way to read the Bible is relationally, as a way of keeping company with Jesus.

What might this look like? How does it work?

For starters, it may slow down our reading because the goal isn't finishing a chapter but rather listening to the Author. It may take us to unexpected places. For example, if we encounter the verses above, we might pause to ask prayerful questions: "Lord, am I reading to draw closer to you? Or for a different reason?" We might confess: "Lord, I feel like I'm missing the forest for the trees." We might ask, "Jesus, you are standing right before me, so please show me what I'm missing. Draw me closer to you. Help me to receive from you the life I want."

Reading the Bible relationally, as a way of listening to God, can draw us closer to God as quickly and as powerfully as anything else we might do. But it's not the only way to listen.

Listen for His Voice

Mary Magdalene stood in the garden, crying. Her hopes had been dashed. Her Rabbi—and friend—had been cruelly executed and hurriedly buried. And now, now, she found His tomb empty. She couldn't imagine who would do such a thing, to steal His body and—it was unimaginable. She stooped to look into the tomb again, as though her eyes had deceived her, and she saw two men in dazzling white robes sitting on either end of the burial slab.

"Woman, why are you crying?" one of them said.

She answered. "They have taken my Lord away, and I don't know where they have put him." She heard the sounds of movement behind her and turned.

A man had approached. "Woman, why are you crying? Who is it you are looking for?"

She wiped her eyes. "Sir, if you have carried him away, tell me where you have put him, and I will get him."

Then the man spoke her name. "Mary." It was Jesus.

"Rabboni!" She stepped toward Him, dropped to her knees, and reached out her arms toward Him.

Jesus said, "Do not hold on to me, for I have not yet ascended to the Father. Go instead to my brothers and tell them, 'I am ascending to my Father and your Father, to my God and your God'" (John 20:11–17).

What a fascinating account—and also one that may help us draw closer to Jesus, as we draw from it a few tips for listening to the Savior's voice in prayer and deepening our relationship with Him.

Expect Him to speak. In her grief and confusion, Mary apparently never expected Jesus to appear and speak to her, so when He did speak, she didn't recognize His voice. How often do we miss the voice of Jesus because we simply don't expect it? How much more often might we hear from Him if we learn to live in a state of anticipation, in which we invite and expect Him to speak?

Get quiet. Gardens tend to be beautifully quiet in the early morning, and we may infer that such was the case for Mary. The angels spoke. She spoke. But other sounds? We don't know, of course, but it seems unlikely that Mary was distracted by talking heads on the television or songs pulsing from her smartphone. We may not start each day in a garden, but we can turn off the radio on our commute or silence notifications on our phone from time to time. Perhaps if we're more often quiet we will more frequently hear the voice of our Lord.

Listen for your name. Evidently, the sound of her name prompted Mary to recognize the risen Jesus. He didn't have to say, "It's me, Jesus!" He simply spoke her name. Similarly, your Lord knows you. The Shepherd calls to you. He knows when to shout and when to whisper. He knows whether to speak your name through a song or a sigh, a breeze or a bruise. As we live in expectation, listening for His voice in our hearts and minds through the ebb and flow of our daily lives, we'll become more attuned to the sound of His voice, and the ways He speaks our names.

Respond with affection and obedience. Many students and scholars have offered explanations for why Jesus told Mary not to hold onto Him, but it may have simply been this: He had a task for her to do. So, when we hear the voice of Jesus in our hearts and minds, we should be ready to respond not only with affection but also with obedience. If we intend to hear His voice and then decide whether or not we will heed it, we're far less likely to hear from Him.

Mary, of course, was practiced in listening to Jesus. How many times had she heard Him speak or teach or laugh? So it will be with us. As we read the Bible relationally, we will become more adept at hearing the Shepherd's voice, whether He ever speaks audibly or not. Our hearts and minds will be tuned to His frequency, so to speak.

Recognize God Speaking Through Others

According to John's gospel, Jesus entrusted to Mary the task of announcing His resurrection to His followers. They first heard that glorious news from her. Likewise, trusted Christian friends, leaders, and counselors can often be the means God uses to speak to us, to answer questions, and to carry on conversations with Him that began in prayer or Bible reading.

For years, I've met with an accountability partner each week. We talk, laugh, and sometimes cry together. But we also do as James advised when he wrote, "confess your sins to each other and pray for each other so that you may be healed" (James 5:16). And when we do, one of us will say to the other, "I tell you in Jesus's name, you are forgiven." Hearing the grace of our Lord Jesus Christ in those words often prompts such deep gratitude that one or both of us is brought to tears.

Of course, it may take trial and error to discern who God chooses and uses to speak to you. Not everyone—not even every Christian—is on God's wavelength, or yours. But wise, prayerful, biblical counsel from a few trustworthy friends can often be the whisper (or megaphone) of God to your soul.

If you really want to know someone, and get to know that person better, you don't just talk, "as one speaks to a friend" (Exodus 33:11), you also listen. Learning to read God's Word relationally, listening for the voice of Jesus in our hearts and minds, and recognizing God's way of speaking to us through others will invariably help us to draw closer and closer to God, and Him to us.

Lord, forgive me for all the praying, reading, and talking I have done without listening for your voice, even when you have called my name. I want to do better at making my relationship with you a two-way street. I want to hear your voice in the precious words of Scripture, in both silences and storms, and through the words of others who enjoy close relationships with you. Help me to read relationally, to tune my heart to your whispers and shouts, and to recognize your way of speaking to me through others. In Jesus's name, amen.

CHAPTER SEVEN

GREAT FAITH . . . UNTIL IT ISN'T

A dear friend of mine was recently interviewed for a job promotion. She asked me and others to pray. We did.

This woman was more than qualified for the job—I couldn't imagine anyone being more suited, nor more worthy of every confidence. After a couple rounds of interviews, she was one of two finalists. So we kept praying.

You probably know where this is going.

She didn't get the job.

I was sure she would get it. She was sure she would be chosen. A whole bunch of praying people were sure she'd be hired, but she wasn't.

I hate that. I mean, we prayed, right? She surrendered the whole thing to God. She trusted Him for the outcome. And she was disappointed. Sorely disappointed. She wrote me afterward, "I thought when you surrendered it all to God and let go, He was supposed to give it back to you—not just say—OK, I'm taking it, you can't have it."

Most of us don't like uncertainty. We want sure things. We require safety and surety. We want a "money-back guarantee," and we think someone's at fault and someone should pay if anything goes wrong. We want wealth without risk, truth without consequences, gain without pain. But as much as I hate to admit it, that's no way to get closer to God.

Walk This Way

The followers of Jesus had to be riding a spiritual high following the miraculous feeding of the multitude. Thousands of hungry people had been fed with a single boy's simple lunch. They also could have been worn out from the demanding organization, distribution, and collection process surrounding that event, like the exhaustion that follows volunteering for vacation Bible school. So, understandably,

Immediately Jesus made the disciples get into the boat and go on ahead of him to the other side, while he dismissed the crowd. After he had dismissed them, he went up on a mountainside by himself to pray. Later that night, he was there alone, and the boat was already a considerable distance from land, buffeted by the waves because the wind was against it. Shortly before dawn Jesus went out to them, walking on the lake. (Matthew 14:22–25)

It was called "the fourth watch," between 3 and 6 a.m. That was the time "shortly before dawn," referenced in the passage above. And it came after a f-u-l-l day. A day of exertion and exhaustion and crowds and miracles and adrenaline highs and lows. And now, in the black of night, Jesus's disciples were *still* in the boat, trying to make their way across the lake. It was eight miles at its widest point, but a difficult wind and rollicking waves kept the boys from getting to the other side. And Matthew— or Levi, which was his Hebrew name—reports so matter-of-factly,

"And then, you know, Jesus came walking on the water."

(At least that's the way I read it!)

To be fair, those words were written years later, after Matthew had seen Jesus rise from the dead and ascend to heaven, so maybe something like walking on water was old hat by the time this was written (and, to be even more fair, many of us would admit that the longer we walk with Jesus, the more extraordinary things become routine). But Jesus's followers weren't yet experienced in the whole "water-walking Messiah" thing.

They freaked: "When the disciples saw him walking on the lake, they were terrified. 'It's a ghost,' they said, and cried out in fear" (Matthew 14:26).

Now, we should probably keep a couple things in mind. Some of these guys were sailors, and even in those days, sailors could be a somewhat superstitious lot. But also, it was between 3 and 6 in the morning and the account says that from the time "evening came"—around sunset—until sometime between 3 and 6 a.m. their fishing boat had been buffeted by angry waves.

So, they're a little superstitious anyway, they're dog tired, and they're in a crazy storm. In a situation like that, maybe you'd scream like a ninny, too. Maybe not.

But after the disciples saw Jesus,

But Jesus immediately said to them: "Take courage! It is I. Don't be afraid."

"Lord, if it's you," Peter replied, "tell me to come to you on the water."

"Come," he said.

Then Peter got down out of the boat, walked on the water and came toward Jesus. But when he saw the wind, he was afraid and, beginning to sink, cried out, "Lord, save me!"

Immediately Jesus reached out his hand and caught him. "You of little faith," he said, "why did you doubt?" And when they climbed into the boat, the wind died down.

Then those who were in the boat worshiped him, saying, "Truly you are the Son of God." (Matthew 14:27–33)

Now, Peter clearly possessed great faith . . . until he didn't. But why did Jesus even let him step out of the boat?

Christ could have said, "No, Peter, you're fine where you are." Why allow Peter to take such a risk? Was it because Jesus was there all along, as He is with you and me? Was it because every step Peter took moved him closer to Jesus, as it might with you and me? Was it because storm or no storm, boat or no boat, Jesus wants us closer to Him even more than we want to be closer to Him?

Common Hindrances

Do you feel more like Peter when he stepped out of the boat, or when he began to sink? When he cried out to Jesus, "Lord, save me," or when he heard Jesus saying, "Faint-heart, what got into you?" (Matthew 14:31 MSG).

We are all Peter, in a way. We have our moments of faith and boldness, but we're also often tripped up in our efforts to get closer to the Master. Some of the most common hindrances are temptation, sin, fear, and legalism, so let's talk about them a little more specifically.

Temptation. We shouldn't be surprised to be tempted, no matter how strongly we long to be closer to God. But temptation isn't sin; even Jesus was tempted, though He never sinned. In fact, we may experience greater temptation as we get closer to God.

Did the wind and waves around Peter become stronger as he made his way toward Jesus? Maybe not, but "The temptations in your life are no different from what others experience. And God is faithful. He will not allow the temptation to be more than you can stand. When you are tempted, he will show you a way out so that you can endure" (1 Corinthians 10:13 NLT).

Sin. The same Peter who walked on water later denied ever knowing Jesus, even after the Lord had warned him that was going to happen (see Luke 22:31–32). Our response to temptation will either drive us closer to God or farther from God. If we tolerate temptation or, worse, flirt with it, we strengthen the temptation rather than ourselves.

Listen, sin will always distance us from God, while humility, repentance, and obedience will always draw us closer to Him. The hope, of course, is "that [we] will not sin. But if anybody does sin, we have an advocate with the Father—Jesus Christ, the Righteous One" (1 John 2:1). And we can find assurance and confidence in the realization that the same Jesus who prayed for and restored Peter "is also interceding for us" (Romans 8:34).

Fear. Peter's fear of sinking and drowning produced doubt during a moment that might have been a moment of great blessing and beauty for him on the Sea of Galilee. His fear of ridicule and perhaps capture, imprisonment, and death may have been the reason he denied even knowing Jesus in the courtyard of the high priest after Jesus was arrested. Similarly, our fears can trip us and prevent us from being as close to God as we want to be.

What if God calls me as a missionary? What if I turn into one of those "weird" Christians who can't shut up about God? Will I have to give up my dream of playing drums in a heavy metal rock band?

Our fears don't even have to be reasonable—and they usually aren't. But when we recognize them and confess them, we are better able to "draw near to God with a sincere heart and with the full assurance that faith brings" (Hebrews 10:22).

Legalism. Like Peter, the most vocal disciple in pledging his devotion to Jesus, those who long to be closer with God are sometimes persuaded to think, "If I do everything just right, God will accept me and show me favor." Such an attitude, however, often produces a definition of "right" that neglects humility, repentance, and grace. It replaces those Christlike virtues with pride, arrogance, and judgmentalism. Jesus contrasted humble virtue and legalistic pride in one of His most powerful stories:

> To some who were confident of their own righteousness and looked down on everyone else, Jesus told this parable: "Two men went up to the temple to pray, one a Pharisee and the other a tax collector. The Pharisee stood by himself and prayed: 'God, I thank you that I am not like other people—robbers, evildoers,

adulterers—or even like this tax collector. I fast twice a week and give a tenth of all I get.'

"But the tax collector stood at a distance. He would not even look up to heaven, but beat his breast and said, 'God, have mercy on me, a sinner.'

"I tell you that this man, rather than the other, went home justified before God. For all those who exalt themselves will be humbled, and those who humble themselves will be exalted." (Luke 18:9–14)

As Jesus's story depicts, there may be nothing quite like confession, as well as prayers of gratitude, that prevents the stumbling block of legalism in our lives. The closer we get to God, the more aware we will become of our own need to pray, "God, have mercy on me, a sinner"—and the more frequent will be our prayers of thanks for God's great mercy and grace toward us.

That attitude, in turn, may just draw us closer to our Lord, step by step, and—storm or no storm, boat or no boat—keep us from sinking.

Lord, have mercy on me, a sinner.

Save me from the winds and waves that impede my efforts to get closer to you.

Steer me away from temptation, even as you remind me that temptation isn't sin—and may even be more intense as I draw closer to you.

I know that Satan would sift me like wheat and draw me into sin, and therefore farther from you, so please make humility, repentance, and obedience my daily diet.

Deliver me from fear, whether reasonable or unreasonable, that prevent me from drawing near to you with a sincere heart and with the full assurance that faith brings.

Protect me from legalistic pride, arrogance, and judgmentalism; make me quick to recognize and confess my own sin, and gracious and kind toward others whose temptations and struggles look different from mine.

Draw me, step by step, and—storm or no storm, boat or no boat—take my hand and keep me from sinking.

CHAPTER EIGHT

TAKING TIME TO TRIBE

Dewey was two years old when his father died. His mother lived with several different men after that; none were husbands, and none exhibited the slightest fatherly interest in Dewey. It was clear to him that he was an inconvenience to his mother—sometimes an outright nuisance. A burden.

For a while, Dewey was passed from one family member to another. Some tolerated him. Some abused him. None wanted him.

When he was seven years old, a family adopted him. Good news, right?

Except that roughly a year later, the family took him back to his mother, explaining that they didn't like him and didn't see how it could ever work.

By the time he was eight years old, Dewey could find no reason to believe anyone could ever accept him, care for him, love him. He possessed no hope that there was anywhere he would fit in. Ever.

But then, right around his ninth birthday, Dewey was adopted by a family named Hughes. He says, "In Mr. Hughes, I found unconditional love. Finally, I had a lap to crawl up into and feel safe and protected and loved. Within a few days, I was calling him 'Dad.' Why? Because he loved me, and made me feel safe. I grew to love him because he loved me. What I needed at that time, my dad gave me."

And that, says the man I know today as my friend, Dewey Hughes, is what he found in God through Jesus.

"God gave me an unconditional love, a place of safety, a salvation, a peace, and a life in His kingdom. I grew more and more in love with God because of what He added to me. Each day, I discover more that He adds to me, and I grow a little more in love. I discover more holes and empty places in my life that only He can fill. How can you not accept someone who so graciously accepts you?"[1]

If Dewey had never known his adoptive father's love, could he have understood and accepted his heavenly Father's love? If he hadn't become a "Hughes," would he ever have experienced a sense of belonging? If he hadn't found his "tribe," so to speak, would he be a follower of Jesus (and pastor) today? Would he be as close to God as he is?

We can't know the answers to those questions, of course, but they're worth pondering. One of the ways we hinder our pursuit of a closer relationship with God is by trying to make the trip on our own. We see our spiritual lives as solo performances, and in so doing we make things more difficult than they have to be.

Don't Go It Alone

None of us is an island, as the poet (and pastor) John Donne said.[2] And drawing near to God is not a solely individual pursuit; the journey is fueled by community. It's made easier and better when we find and connect with people who share our personalities, purposes, values, and goals. Sadly, many people never find a place to belong, so their efforts to draw near to God are more difficult than they might be otherwise. They may have had an emotional connection, a sexual connection, or intellectual connection with someone; they may have had college friends, drinking buddies, or dinner companions, but never a heart-to-heart, soul-to-soul connection with others who are heading the same direction, passionate about the same things, and moving closer and closer to God. There may be many reasons for this, but three come quickly to mind:

1. *Time.* You hear it all the time: "I'll catch up with you later." "We have to get together—soon!" "I can't believe how long it's been!" "Have your people call my people." We feel too busy to develop meaningful relationships, let alone find and develop a tribe that will foster and encourage our pursuit of a closer relationship with God. "There just aren't enough hours in the day."

2. *Technology.* These days we can order a book, shop for clothes, see our grandkid's latest photo, play a four-person game of Scrabble, exchange ideas with a half dozen people, conduct a business meeting, and schedule a flight, hotel, and car rental without ever coming into personal, face-to-face, eyeball-to-eyeball contact with another living, breathing human being. We can do it all online! We love email,

Amazon, Wikipedia. But communication, shopping, and research used to involve contact with other human beings. Now, as a result of modern technology, day after day goes by and our need for relationships that support a closer relationship with God becomes more and more acute.

3. *Trust*. Or, more accurately, the lack of it. Some of us have been hurt, and hurt deeply. And computers don't hurt us, televisions don't hurt us, books don't hurt us. People do. And churches do, because they're made up of people. So of course we hold back and make sure no one ever does it again. But circling the wagons, so to speak, and protecting ourselves from the dangers of human contact also insulates us from the blessings of a closer relationship with God, because He has designed us to need the encouragement and inspiration of others in pursuing a closer relationship with Him.

But how? How can we do that? As in anything, we start by asking God for help ("You do not have because you do not ask God," as James 4:2 says). Ask Him to help you overcome whatever obstacles hinder you from finding and enjoying your tribe.

efining Your Tribe

If we look closely at the life of Jesus as recorded in the Gospels, the four books that tell the story of Jesus's life and ministry, we might see that Jesus intentionally cultivated three circles of relationships, and they contributed in different ways to His relationship with God and others.

Even Jesus didn't know everybody. Though He was also God, as a human being, He had only so many hours in a day. He could be in only one place at a time. But as He began to preach and teach, there arose a first circle of friends and followers that apparently numbered seventy or so, whom Jesus probably knew from school, church (the synagogue, actually), and His hometown or the surrounding area. He thought highly enough of these people that He commissioned them to be His representatives, sending them out in pairs to do ministry in His name (see Luke 10).

From that circle of friends, He gathered a second, smaller circle, whom we might call His close friends, a group we know today as The Twelve. This diverse group of friends signed up as His *talmidim*, or students.[3] They learned from Him, traveled with Him, ran errands for Him, and eventually were also sent out to work miracles and spread the news of

God's kingdom all over the countryside (see Ma.
6, Luke 9).

Within that circle of close friends was an even
smaller, third circle made up of Peter, James, and
John, people whom we might call His intimate
friends. One of them even called himself "the disciple whom Jesus loved." Those three hardly ever
left Jesus's side. They accompanied Jesus into the
room where He raised Jairus's daughter from the
dead (while the other nine waited outside). They
went up the mountain with Him, where they saw
Him transfigured and watched Him talk with Moses
and Elijah (while the other nine waited below). They
also attended Jesus in the Garden of Gethsemane,
where He sought their support as He wrestled in
prayer, contemplating His coming trial and execu-
tion (while the other nine waited farther away).
Peter, James, and John encouraged, challenged, supported, and protected Him more than any of the
others (see John 21:20, Mark 9:18–26, Matthew
17:1–13, and Luke 22:39–46).

If Jesus needed and enjoyed those three distinct
levels of relationships, maybe we do too. Maybe
defining and refining those kinds of friendships will
make a difference in our spiritual lives. If we can
identify and develop like-minded and like-hearted
friends who also long to be closer to God, maybe

can learn from each other and—like Jesus and His friends—experience heights together that we couldn't have scaled alone.

Refining Your Tribe

Your circle of friends may currently look nothing like Jesus's relationships. That's okay. Your closest friends currently may not be people who share your personality, purpose, values, and goals. That's okay too. If we were already as close to God as we could possibly get, we wouldn't need anything or anyone. It's a process, even a fun one. Let's start with the three concentric circles.

Take a sheet of paper and draw three concentric circles of decreasing circumference—one large outer circle, a middle-sized circled placed inside the larger outer one, and a smaller inner circle place inside the middle one.

Before reading on to the next chapter, preferably in the next day or two, write in the large outer circle the names of your extended group of friends. They don't have to number seventy, as Jesus's larger circle did, but you might include friends from school, church, and your hometown or the surrounding area. More than acquaintances, these are the people you would call if you threw a party.

In the middle circle, write the names of twelve or so close friends. These are the people you've kept track of, people you've stayed in touch with, people you could call for a small loan. (It's OK if there are not quite twelve people in this list yet.)

In the centermost circle, write the names of your intimates. It's okay if there is only one or two, instead of three. These are the people you would call to bail you out of jail or to take you in for a few nights when your water or air conditioning breaks down, or to sit in silence with you by your spouse's death bed.

Chances are, unless your life is overflowing with good relationships, one or more of those circles is going to seem out of whack. You may have lots of friends like Jesus did, but only one close friend and no real intimates. Or you may have a few intimate friends, but not many friends in the middle or outer circles. The numbers themselves aren't all that important, but it's crucial that your closest friends be like-minded and like-hearted people who long to be closer to God, as you do.

If you don't have many close friends or intimates, try looking at your outer circle of friends and identify people in that group you want to get to know better. Circle or underline those names, and intentionally look for ways to develop that relationship.

Does that person like coffee? Invite him to Star-bucks. Does she attend or lead a Bible study? Ask if you can join in. Don't become a stalker but do intentionalize relationships that have the potential to become close, like-minded friends. And be pre-pared for a process of trial-and-error; not everyone is a kindred spirit, and some who are kindred spir-its will move away—or you will. That's okay, just keep working the circles and adding (or subtracting) names, until you're enjoying a few relationships that propel you closer and closer to God.

What if you don't have enough people in your outermost circle of friends? Or what if they're all jerks? Or they all live in Saskatchewan? Then look for ways to widen that circle, until it contains some people you would really like to get to know.

You might look for a church, small group, book club, community center, or volunteer orga-nization—or start your own. Invite others to a neighborhood Bible study, cycling group, or cook-ing class, and see what develops. The goal is to meet people who in three years or five years or even ten years will be a best friend, prayer partner, accountability partner, coffee buddy, or a Peter, James, and John, who understands and encourages your pursuit of a closer and stronger relationship with God.

So what're you waiting for? Ask God for His help. Pick up the phone. Make a call or send out a text. Put something on your calendar. And give God the chance to use others as catalysts to move you closer to Him.

Jesus, thank you for the vivid example you provided of circles of constructive relationships that foster spiritual vitality.

Please make me alert to people who share my personality, purpose, values, and goals. Point me to them, and them to me.

And please grant me wisdom and sensitivity to cultivate friendships—especially close friendships—that will be catalysts in my quest to draw closer to you. Amen.

CHAPTER NINE

NOT ENOUGH

Are you doing enough?

Praying enough? Reading your Bible enough? Attending church? Giving? Everything else?

Is "not doing enough" the reason you're not as close to God as you'd like to be? Is that what you think? If so, then have I got good news for you!

First of all, you're not alone. You're not the only one who tends to think that way. Others among us, when we feel dissatisfied with our spiritual lives, reflexively chalk it up to "not doing enough." And well-meaning people around us are often happy to encourage such thoughts. They say, "You know what you need to do? Get on your face before God." Or "You just need to read the Bible more." Or "Have you been missing church lately?" Or "If you're feeling distant from God, guess who moved?"

And there's some truth to those sentiments. There are definitely actions we can take that create distance between us and God, and other actions that foster intimacy with God. But over time, we get the message that we're not doing "enough." So we try harder. We get up earlier. We do more. We add to our already heavy daily load, in the hope of fixing our problem. If we can just do "enough," we can find the fulfillment and satisfaction we crave.

But that idea doesn't come from Jesus.

Enough vs. Easy

In Jesus's day, when a student decided to enroll in the school of a particular rabbi, he was said to take the rabbi's "yoke," a reference to the wooden beam used to connect a pair of oxen or other animals together so they would pull a wagon or plow in the same direction.[1] It pictured the student walking the same way as the teacher, side-by-side, step-by-step. And many of the rabbis up to and including the time of Jesus placed heavy restrictions and demands on their followers. Though one rabbi's "yoke" differed from another's, all tended to equate closeness to God with doing all of the right things and not doing any of the wrong things—doing "enough."[2]

And then came Jesus. He said,

> "Come to me, all you who are weary and burdened, and I will give you rest. Take my yoke upon you and learn from me, for I am gentle and humble in heart, and you will find rest for your souls. For my yoke is easy and my burden is light." (Matthew 11:28–30)

When Jesus said, "my yoke is easy," He referred to the relative ease of going His way, side-by-side and step-by-step. He didn't claim to place no burden at all on His followers, but He did promise a light load, a relief, especially compared to the way of the Pharisees, who were constantly adding "dos" and "don'ts" to people's lives.

Jesus doesn't say, "you're not doing enough." He doesn't say "try harder." He says, "Come . . . and I will give you rest." That promise is for you and me too. If we come to Jesus and don't feel at rest, then it's not His "yoke" we've taken. If we come to Him and feel stressed and pressed to do more, it's not His way we're going.

When you think of your spiritual life, do you think, "I'm not doing enough"? Or do you think, "my burden is light; my soul is at rest"?

Doing vs. Being

Those earliest followers of Jesus didn't have many of the things we enjoy today. They had no conferences or concerts to attend. They couldn't download prayer podcasts or wear Christian t-shirts. They didn't even have personal Bibles! But they seem to have been energized by a "new and living way" of life that kept them close to God and to each other.

The Bible says that the first generation of Jesus-followers focused on a few simple things: learning from the apostles, gathering in each other's homes, enjoying meals together, and praying (see Acts 2:42). They also shared financially and materially with each other, even selling possessions sometimes to help someone in need, bringing the proceeds of the sale to the apostles for distribution. There is no indication that church leaders told people to do this. There seems to have been no giving campaign or sermon series on the subject of generosity. And it's clear that not everyone sold everything; it was apparently just something people did, as they were able and so inclined (see Acts 4:32–37).

But some in the church may have gotten the impression that they weren't doing "enough." They were a married couple named Ananias and Sapphira, and we don't know if they had already tried praying more or going to church more often. But we do know that they thought they needed to increase their giving. Considerably. And flamboyantly.

They "sold a piece of property," the Bible says (Acts 5:1). So far, so good. They didn't *have* to sell anything, but they did. They didn't have to give any of the proceeds to anyone else, but they decided to bring some of the proceeds to the apostles. They didn't have to announce their gift or give the impression that they were donating the whole thing, but they evidently did, because Peter called them on it. Each of them, in turn. He even gave them each the chance to correct the account or impression that they had turned over all of the money to the church, but they didn't.

They lied, and then they stood by their lie. Peter called it lying to the Holy Spirit and, when they were confronted, Ananias and Sapphira each dropped dead.

The whole sordid account of Ananias and Sapphira is recorded in Acts 5:1–11, and much has been said and written about their actions. A lot of it is puzzling. How many churches today would complain if someone made a sizeable contribution, no matter what impression they gave while doing it? Why was the punishment so extreme? Why hasn't their story become a popular vacation Bible school theme ("Lying in church can get you killed")?

But seriously, whatever else went wrong that day, the root of their problem could have been that Ananias and Sapphira felt like they weren't doing "enough." Maybe they admired Barnabas, who seemed to be closer to God and more esteemed by others. Maybe the amount they gave was calculated to be a little more than what Barnabas had given so they could exceed his gift and still buy new drapes for the house. Part of the problem with "not enough" is that no one tells you what "enough" is.

Except for Jesus.

His words in Matthew 11:28–30 say to me, "Don't worry about doing 'enough.' That can be deadly. It's not about doing; it's about being. It's not about performance, it's about a person—me. Just be with me. Walk with me. Come this way. Watch and learn. Take one step at a time, side-by-side with me, and learn to live in the freedom and blessing I've purchased for you."

Failure vs. Freedom

Ananias's and Sapphira's efforts didn't get them closer to God, and neither will our attempts to "do enough" today. Falling into the performance trap—"I have to pray more," "I need to read the Bible more," "I should probably get my name on the Giving Tree in the church lobby"—will end in failure, not freedom. That's why it's called a trap.

And that's why the one-time Pharisee, Paul of Tarsus, fairly harped on the subject of our freedom from "unbearable religious demands" (Matthew 23:4 NLT). He wrote, "Where the Spirit of the Lord is, there is freedom" (2 Corinthians 3:17). And, "It is for freedom that Christ has set us free. Stand firm, then, and do not let yourselves be burdened again by a yoke of slavery" (Galatians 5:1).

We're more likely to feel distant from God if we take on a yoke that's not easy and a burden that's not light, because then it's not *Jesus* we're yoked to, and it's not *His* way we're following. It is most likely our own.

We may pull as hard as we like in the direction of "doing enough" to please God and draw closer to Him, but if we're focused on simply being with Jesus, spending time with Him—whatever that looks like in this life today—we can learn to live in the freedom and blessing He purchased for us.

If we'll live in that freedom, He'll draw us closer to His side than we could ever get by "doing enough."

Lord, help me not to make the mistake of thinking I'm not "doing enough."

Help me to focus on simply being with you, walking with you, side-by-side, day by day, a step at a time.

Teach me to live in the freedom and blessing you purchased for me. Draw me closer to your side than I could ever get by "doing enough." Amen.

CHAPTER TEN

MORE FROM GOD

Two seas.

A mere hundred miles apart.

But they could hardly be more different.

One is a scene of beauty, a center of commerce and tourism whose shores and depths teem with life. Fish abound in its waters, more than twenty different varieties. Grass carpets its slopes. The surrounding countryside is a patchwork of thriving villages and valued farmland.

The other sea's shores are barren, the atmosphere harsh, and its depths devoid of plant and animal life except for sulfide-eating bacteria and microbial fungi. Its waters can't quench thirst; they would poison anything that drinks them.

The difference is in the flow.

The Dead Sea receives fresh water daily from the Jordan River and other small springs under and around it, but it hoards everything it gets. All the minerals halt their flow within its boundaries, and there they remain, except for asphalt, which the Dead Sea constantly spits up from the deep seeps onto its shores.

The Sea of Galilee, however, sparkles with freshness because it not only receives the water that flows down from the mountains to its north, but also gives itself day after day, moment-by-moment, to the winding Jordan River as it flows to the south.[1]

That principle applies to people too.

Contagious Grace

If there was ever a man like the Dead Sea, it was him. He lived and worked in Jericho, a town not far from the salty shores. He oversaw the collection of taxes for the Roman occupiers, and skimmed and extorted great wealth from his neighbors in the process. He knew everyone despised him, but he didn't care. He may have been one of the shortest men in town too, but so what? He was also the richest.

One morning, he heard Jesus, the healer and prophet from Galilee was approaching with His band of followers. Zacchaeus dropped everything to go see the Galilean that had cause so much chattering. By the time he got there, crowds already lined the street, hip-to-hip and shoulder-to-shoulder. They blocked his view, many of them rudely and intentionally. It became a sport to some, who found his frustration entertaining. The noise of the crowd signaled the approaching entourage, but Zacchaeus would not be defeated. Maybe a boy's legs dangling from the branch of a sprawling sycamore tree gave him the idea. He climbed up.

He smiled. His view was better than anyone else's, and just in time.

The teacher approached, stopped, and looked up.

"Zacchaeus, come down immediately. I must stay at your house today."

Every head in the crowd turned. Not only had Jesus spoken directly to the tax collector; He had called him by name. Zacchaeus scrambled to the ground and the crowd parted for him.

He led the way to his lavish home and, working alongside his own servants, quickly prepared a feast for the teacher and His followers. Some of the town's residents even straggled in. Jesus reclined on the couch closest to Zacchaeus while the others spread out like spokes from a wheel, and throughout the meal the tax collector felt his heart strangely warmed by the man's kindness and ease in his company. He had forgotten what it felt like to be treated with anything but hatred and disgust.

Suddenly Zacchaeus stood, and the room quieted. He removed the rings from his fingers and set them on the low table in front of Jesus. "Look, Lord! Here and now I give half of my possessions to the poor." He placed his hand on his heart as if to control his emotions. "And if I have cheated anybody out of anything—" He smiled, belatedly acknowledging the ludicrous dishonesty of his word, *if.* "I will pay back four times the amount."

Jesus fixed him with a gaze and then slowly scanned the faces around the low table, as everyone awaited the teacher's reaction. "Today," He said, "salvation has come to this house, because this man, too, is a son of Abraham. For the Son of Man came to seek and to save the lost."[2]

Givers and Takers

There are two kinds of people in the world: givers, and takers. Zacchaeus had always been a taker, but the closer he got to Jesus—when he experienced the mercy, grace, and "the love of God that is in

Christ Jesus our Lord" (Romans 8:39)—kindness
and generosity started to flow from him. It reminds
me of something Andrew Murray wrote:

> Wherever there is life, there is a continual in-
> terchange of taking in and giving out, receiv-
> ing and restoring. The nourishment I take is
> given out again in the work I do; the impres-
> sions I receive, in the thoughts and feelings I
> express. The one depends on the other—the
> giving out ever increases the power of taking
> in. In the healthy exercise of giving and taking
> is all the enjoyment of life.
>
> It is so in the spiritual life too. There are
> Christians who look on its blessedness as con-
> sisting all in the privilege of ever receiving;
> they know not how the capacity for receiving is
> only kept up and enlarged by continual giving
> up and giving out—how it's only in the empti-
> ness that comes from the parting with what we
> have, that the divine fullness can flow in. It was
> a truth our Saviour continually insisted on.[3]

Are takers stale, unpleasant, and bitter because
they're far from God? Or do they become more
distant from God because they're stale, unpleasant,
and bitter? The answer is yes. Likewise, men and

women who freely give of themselves—their time, possessions, emotions, and lives—seem to find it easier to draw closer to God. And those who draw closer to God find it easier to be generous.

The wise king, Solomon, once said, "One person gives freely, yet gains even more; another withholds unduly, but comes to poverty. A generous person will prosper; whoever refreshes others will be refreshed" (Proverbs 11:24–25).

It's not a linear equation (if you're generous, you will be close to God) but a cycle (closeness to God produces generosity which draws you closer to God, and so on). It's not a deal God makes with people, along the lines of, "Plant a seed to feed your greed." It's just that those who give more of themselves to others mysteriously (miraculously?) discover that there's also more of God to receive.

The principle has been dramatized many times. You remember Charles Dickens's *A Christmas Carol*. It's the story of an old miser, Ebenezer Scrooge, who receives a series of ghostly visitors. The three spirits of Christmas show him what his selfishness and greed do—not only to others, but also to him. When the ghosts leave, he finally begins to share his wealth with others, and finds the results so thrilling, so exhilarating, that he suddenly can't give enough!

In a lesser known story, George Eliot's *Silas Marner*, the title character is a lonely, embittered old man who spends his evenings counting and recounting his hoard of gold coins, until two strange events occur, one right after the other. First, he is robbed of his gold coins. Second, an unknown baby girl appears practically on his doorstep. He takes in the little girl, and names her Eppie. And he begins to change. As he starts to care for the child and give to someone other than himself, a transformation occurs. The more he gives, the richer he becomes.

Such stories aren't found only in fiction.

Take ninety-three-year-old Cecil Green, for instance. My brother met Cecil at a convention for fundraisers. Cecil had given away more money than most people ever see in their lifetimes. He'd given millions of dollars to various organizations, and he was invited to this particular convention to receive an award for all the good things his generosity had accomplished.

As he reached the top of the wobbly steps to the podium, he shook loose from the people who supported his ninety-three-year-old form and walked toward the podium. With each step he seemed to get more excited and energetic, until suddenly he stopped, looked at the crowd, and broke into a dance that looked something like an Irish jig.

Then he stepped to the podium. "I am so excited and I appreciate this award very much. But I don't understand why someone should be given such an award for doing something so enjoyable. Giving away my money is so much fun I wish everyone could do it. My goal is to be able to give everything away before I die."[4]

Cecil Green had spent much of his life working hard to earn as much as he could. While he enjoyed making money, he didn't really start to have fun until he started giving it away! The more he gave away, it seemed, the more fun he had.

We don't have to be rich to give as though we were. Doug, a friend of mine from church, told me of a late-night phone call he once received. It was an old friend of his calling from several time zones away. While Doug tried to shake off sleep, his friend explained that years earlier, he'd resolved never to let a day go by without giving something away. It might be a quarter to some kid who lost his money in a vending machine or a book to someone he knew would enjoy a good read. And he had called that night, he said, to give Doug something. He remembered something Doug had done for him years before, and wanted to tell him how much that gesture had meant to him. He gave him a compliment and his heartfelt thanks, and then hung up the phone.

Another story comes by way of reporter Anne Keegan in the *Chicago Tribune Magazine*.[5] It's about George, a homeless man who slept at the YMCA most nights. He owned only the clothes he wore: a shirt, a pair of pants, a pair of shoes wrapped with rubber bands to keep the soles from flapping, and a shabby coat.

On cold winter days, George would go to the police station nearby and spend the morning sitting in an old metal chair in the back. At least it was warm there.

A couple police officers befriended George. They would occasionally slip him a few dollars for a cup of coffee, as would Billy, a nearby restaurant owner, who also gave George a hot breakfast every morning, for no charge. The officers decided to invite George to join their families for Christmas dinner, and George agreed. They even gave him a few presents, which he unwrapped carefully and gratefully.

As they drove back to the YMCA that evening, George asked, "Are these presents really mine . . . to keep?" When the officers nodded, George asked the officers to drive by Billy's restaurant before taking him home.

By the time they arrived at Billy's restaurant, George had carefully rewrapped all his presents.

He tucked them under his arms and walked into the restaurant.

He addressed the man behind the counter. "You've always been real good to me, Billy. Now I can be good to you." He plopped the presents down on the counter and slid them toward Billy. "Merry Christmas!" he said, as he gave away all of his newfound wealth.

"One person gives freely, yet gains even more," Proverbs 11:24 tells us. Andrew Murray adds, "It is only in the emptiness that comes from the parting with what we have, that the divine fullness can flow in."[6] When we live in that flow, that cycle, we'll more likely enjoy fresh encounters with God, coming and going, around and around, and where it stops—nobody knows.

God, please help me to live in that "flow." Teach me to be a giver rather than a taker, to freely share the mercy, grace, and blessings that you have given to me—not for the purpose of gaining more, but with the understanding that you are constantly generous, giving more of yourself to those who give more of themselves. Make me like you, in this and in every respect, in Jesus's name, amen.

CONCLUSION

You feel oddly at peace.

Enthused. Expectant.

And you wonder if you're the only one. You're sitting in church, looking around, eager for the service to begin. A woman catches your glance, and you smile. She smiles back, and you close your eyes and inhale deeply, contentedly.

It doesn't seem like that long ago that you sat in this very spot and felt uneasy, as though others in the room were enjoying a closeness with God that you craved but couldn't claim. Not that you don't want to be still closer, more vibrant in your spiritual life. You'll probably always want to go deeper, know Him better, experience Him more.

You open your eyes, and see the row of green, leafy plants that line the platform, a few of which look as though they're about to bloom. Then you notice one plant, the next-to-the-last on the right side. It's blooming, delicate white petals bravely peeking out atop a slender stem, reaching upward, as if in prayer. You stare, transfixed, wondering if anyone else has noticed it, wondering if anyone else identifies with it as strongly as you do. You feel as though your soul is emerging from a long dormancy, and you're hopeful and keen to keep growing Godward.

You know, of course, that your spiritual life hasn't become suddenly perfect. Not by a long shot. But something's different. You've made great strides. You've set aside some things that had been holding you back. Instead of feeling guilty about your prayer life, you're keeping company with Jesus, and some of the conversations the two of you have together are blowing your mind. You've never been so eager to open your Bible as you are now. Your closest friends are not only aware of your quest, but they share your desire to grow closer and closer to God. You still beat yourself up sometimes, but you're feeling freer and stronger than ever before. You even feel like you're living in the flow, receiving God's love and overflowing with love for those around you. You're amazed. Humbled. And grateful.

Best of all, you're only getting started.

NOTES

Chapter 1

1. Johnson Oatman, Jr., "Higher Ground," public domain.

2. "Glossary: Talmidim," *Psalm11918.org*, accessed October 3, 2018, https://www.psalm11918.org/References/Glossary/talmidim.html.

Chapter 3

1. Thanks to theologian Dallas Willard for this phrase, from his work *The Divine Conspiracy*.

2. Brennan Manning, *The Ragamuffin Gospel* (Sisters, OR: Multnomah, 2000), 24.

Chapter 4

1. "Jesus Fulfilled the Prophet Malachi's Awesome Prophecy of the Tzit-Tzit," *BibleProbe.com*, accessed October 3, 2018, http://www.bibleprobe.com/tzittzit.htm.

2. Quotations from Mark 9:14–27 NIV.

Chapter 5

1. Philip Yancey, *Prayer* (Grand Rapids, MI: Zondervan, 2006), 62.

2. Quoted in J. Oswald Sanders, *Spiritual Leadership* (Chicago: Moody Press, 1994), 86.

3. E. G. Carre, *Praying Hyde: Apostle of Prayer* (Alachua, FL: Bridge-Logos Publishers, 1982), 26.

Chapter 6

1. "Bimah," *Merriam-Webster.com*, accessed October 3, 2018, https://www.merriam-webster.com/dictionary/bimah; and "Gabbai," *Merriam-Webster.com*, accessed October 3, 2018, https://www.merriam-webster.com/dictionary/gabbai.

Chapter 8

1. From an interview by the author with Dewey Hughes.

2. John Donne, *Devotions upon Emergent Occasions and Death's Duel* (New York: Vintage Books, 1999), 103.

3. "Glossary: Talmidim," *Psalm11918.org*, accessed October 3, 2018, https://www.psalm11918.org/References/Glossary/talmidim.html.

Chapter 9

1. Ray Vander Laan, *Echoes of His Presence: Stories of the Messiah from the People of His Day* (Grand Rapids: Zondervan, 1998), introduction, np.

2. See Brad H. Young, *Meet the Rabbis: Rabbinic Thought and the Teachings of Jesus* (Peabody, MA: Hendrickson, 2007), 30ff.

Chapter 10

1. The contrast is drawn from the author's observations on numerous trips to Israel between 1987 and 2010.

2. Quotations from Luke 19:5, 8–10 NIV.

3. Andrew Murray, *Abide in Christ* (Fort Washington, PA: Christian Literature Crusade, 1968), 93.

4. Josh McDowell and Bob Hostetler, *Josh McDowell's One-Year Book of Youth Devotions* (Wheaton, IL: Tyndale, 1997), 145.

5. Anne Keegan, "A Blue Christmas," *Chicago Tribune Magazine,* December 24, 1995.

6. Andrew Murray, op. cit., 93.

ABOUT THE AUTHOR

Bob Hostetler was a teenager working at Camp Swoneky in Ohio when he fully surrendered his life to Jesus—and they've been best friends ever since. Today Bob is an award-winning and best-selling author with more than 4 million copies of his books in print. Some of his favorites include *Don't Check Your Brains at the Door* (with Josh McDowell), *Life Stinks . . . and Then You Die*, and *Take Time to Be Holy*. Find more about this happy camper at BobHostetler.com.